Thai Indian and Chinese Cookbook

Asian Food Made Simple With 210 Tasty Recipes From Thailand India And China

Maki Blanc

CHINESE
COOKBOOK

70 Easy Recipes For
Traditional Food From China

Maki Blanc

The trademarks that are used are without any consent, and the publication of the trademark is without permission or backing by the trademark owner. All trademarks and brands within this book are for clarifying purposes only and are the owned by the owners themselves, not affiliated with this document.

Contents

Introduction

Chinese cuisine (Chinese meals) developed in various parts of Asia and has spread to many other countries. Geographic differences in culture vary widely between China's various regions, resulting in various food styles. There are eight major regional types of food in the United States. In Chinese culture, a meal usually consists of two or more basic elements: the first is a complex carbohydrate or flour, referred to as a staple meal in Chinese, and the second is corresponding dishes of veggies, meat, seafood, or other ingredients.

Most Chinese cuisine relies heavily on rice. On the other hand, Northern China is dominated by wheat-based items such as pasta and steamed bread, while southern China is dominated by rice. In Traditional Chinese, chopsticks are the main feeding utensil for real food, while a large, plain spoon is used for sauces and other fluids. Veganism is not unusual or rare in China, but it is only practiced by a small percentage of the population, as it does in the West.

Many Chinese foods, whether hot or moderate, share a similar base. "The holy trinity of Chinese cuisine is ginger, garlic, and chili. The wok is the core of Chinese cooking and is needed for any stir-fry. There is hardly any limit on the number of traditional meals that can fall out of an unpretentious wok on the cooktop: ginger meat, sticky rice, meat chow fun. The speedy method can preserve nutrients in the veggies while also reducing fuel consumption.

Chinese cuisine is one of the most well-known cooking methods, with a long history and a place among the Chinese cultural resources. It is well-known all over the globe. Chinese cuisine's arrival of Chinese food has evolved over centuries, creating a rich cultural knowledge characterized by a fine selection of ingredients, precise preparation, careful attention to the level of heat, and substantial nourishment.

The evolution and diversity of Chinese cuisine are also a result of China's long history. With each generation, new techniques were made until the craft of food preparation reached its height.

"Chinese Cookbook" is a complete recipe book based on all types of Chinese dishes. It has four chapters with detailed knowledge of the introduction to Chinese cuisine. Recipes from different regions of China are given in each chapter. These chapters are characterized into breakfast, appetizers, snacks, lunch, dinner, desserts, soups, salad, and India's most famous dishes. Try these dishes at your home and make your meals more like Chinese.

Chapter 1: Introduction to Chinese Cuisine

China has a four-thousand-year background, and the People in China have developed a vibrant culture, of which Chinese cuisine is an integral part. The majority of foreign tourists to China are blown away by the country's cuisine. Color, aroma, and taste are all important aspects of Chinese food. Chinese chefs strive to coordinate the colors of their dishes to make them appear more attractive. Some meals are simple, while others are vibrant. A table of Chinese cuisine tends to be very bright and appealing.

The manner Chinese food tastes is extremely significant. Chefs use spices, as well as the components in a recipe, to make food smell healthy. Taste, on the other hand, is the most distinctive attribute of Chinese cuisine. Various methods are used to make Chinese food tasty, providing a great deal of gratification to the palate. Chinese cuisine offers a wide range of material options, which helps Chinese chefs to be more inventive. These involve a variety of grains, fruits, and meat from various animals. The most popular cooking technique is stir-frying. There are eight major divisions of Chinese cuisine. The quality and artistic elegance of Chinese dishes are emphasized in all eight branches.

1.1 History of Chinese Cuisine

Food and its processing have advanced to the point that it is considered an art form in China. People in China, regardless of income, find tasty and healthy meals to be a basic requirement. "Food is the first need of the citizens," says an old Chinese proverb.

Over centuries, this craft has been developed and perfected. According to history, Chinese cuisine first appeared in the 15th century BC during the Shang dynasty but was adopted by Yi Yin, the first Party Leader. Both of China's prevailing ideologies had profound effects on the country's macroeconomic background, but it is less well established that they have shaped the creative arts' growth.

The cultural and intellectual aspects of cooking and eating were significant to Confucius. According to the Chinese, it is considered common manners to bring guests to your home while having enough food. Confucius developed cooking and dinner etiquette codes, the majority of which have survived to this day. The most noticeable instance is slicing bite-sized chunks of meat and veggies during the kitchen's food manufacturing process instead of using a blade at dinner, which is found impolite.

Instead of sampling the different pieces, Confucius advocated combining ingredients and flavorings to create a cohesive dish. His main concern was maintaining harmony. He claimed and demonstrated that there could be no flavor without a combination of ingredients. He also stressed the importance of dish appearance, including color, form, and design. Most notably, preparing became an art rather than a chore, and he was a follower of the concept of "survive to eat" instead of "eat to survive."

On the other side, Tao was a proponent of studies into the nutritional aspects of food and cooking. Taoists were much more concerned with the life-giving kinds of proteins than with their flavor.

For centuries, the Chinese have known that all kinds of roots, herbs, fungi, and crops have medicinal properties. They have told the world that undercooking kills the nutritious value of food, and they have discovered that foods with a good taste also have therapeutic benefits.

1.2 History of Traditional Dishes of Chinese Food

Chinese cuisine has a long tradition, dating back to around 5000 BC. Over such a long period of time, the Chinese have established their distinct method of food preparation. Their methods for recognizing materials to produce optimal blends, multi-phased preparation strategies, and multi-phased flavoring administration have evolved. The ancient Chinese eat a very balanced diet, and we can deduct from historical evidence that agriculture in China began about 5,000 years ago.

Chinese cuisine is known for its diversity and adaptability. Food has been at the center of social communication since prehistoric times, and many modern meals, with their varied aromas and tastes, can be linked back to ancient Chinese food practices. Food has often been regarded as an art form in China, emphasizing the preparation and presentation of food.

Although there were few veggies in ancient China, they were an important part of food types. They consumed veggies with their staple meal, rice, since they could manage it. China is known as one of the world's largest first wine-producing nations. Wine has been endowed with historical and emotional meaning since its creation, representing political and social life and artistic ideas.

Pork, along with other meats such as meat, lamb, duck, chicken, pigeon, and others, is the most popular in China. Pork, which was indigenous to China, was consumed by the Chinese people as early as 4000 or 3000 BC. Tea consumption is regarded as an elegant art form in China, with numerous customs and traditions. Noodles are another traditional Chinese dish. Noodles have a long tradition dating back to the Eastern Han Dynasty.

Agricultural production appears to have played a significant role in China's history, with ancient agricultural activities playing a key role in the country's political, financial, cultural, and ideological advancements.

1.3 Nutritional Information and Benefits of Chinese Food

Chinese food is not only nutrient-dense, but it is also well-balanced, providing all the body and bloodstream need to stay in good shape. The Chinese claim that a significant proportion of veggies and a tiny slice of meat can be fairly designed. Meat is important because it adds refined carbs to the diet. Chinese foods are low in fat, refined carbohydrates, and cholesterol, enabling our bodies to know when they are full. This encourages people who eat Chinese food to consume a more acceptable amount of food and avoid overdoing it on calories. Chinese cuisine also helps to regulate food consumption by emphasizing liquid foods.

According to the yin (cooling wet and moist products) and Yang (heat-producing foods) concepts, all Chinese meals are produced. Almost every dish in Chinese cuisine is prepared with a balance of yin and yang components. Carbohydrates are yin, whereas protein-rich foods are yang. Tea, in general, is well-known for its beneficial effects in treating cardiovascular disease, metabolism, and cancer risk. Chinese chefs haven't forgotten the ancient belief that such ingredients have healing uses.

1.4 Key Ingredients of Chinese Food

Traditional Chinese cuisine achieves its iconic status by creating the perfect balance of spicy, sour, salty, and savory flavors, so you face the risk of disrupting this fine balance by replacing core ingredients. Here is a list of key ingredients used in Chinese cuisine.

- Dried chilies
- Fermented black beans
- White rice vinegar
- Shaoxing rice wine
- Light soy sauce
- Chinese five-spice
- Chili bean sauce
- Dark soy sauce
- Sichuan peppercorns
- Sesame oil
- Dried mushrooms
- Oyster sauce

Chapter 2: Chinese Appetizers Recipes

2.1 Pan-Fried Vegetable Dumplings

Cooking Time: 1 hour
Serving Size: 24 dumplings
Ingredients:
For the Filling
- 24 packaged dumpling skins
- 1 tablespoon vegetable oil
- ¼ teaspoon salt
- 2 teaspoons cornstarch
- ½ cup carrot
- 2 teaspoons soy sauce
- ½ teaspoon pepper powder
- ½ teaspoon sugar
- 2 teaspoons sesame oil
- ½ cup five-spice tofu
- 2 tablespoons minced garlic
- 1 tablespoon scallion whites
- ½ cup seitan
- 1 cup cabbage
- ¼ ounce ear mushrooms

For the Dipping Sauce
- 2 teaspoons rice vinegar
- 1 scallion, sliced
- 4 teaspoons light soy sauce
- 1 teaspoon sesame oil

Method:
1. In a big mixing bowl, mix carrots, cabbage, seitan, mushrooms, broccoli, garlic, spring onion, salt, soy sauce, sesame oil, red pepper, salt, and cornflour.
2. Place a little less than a teaspoon of the fill in the wrap's core to begin sealing the dumpling.
3. Pinch the middle of the wrapper together after folding it in half.
4. In a large nonstick baking pan, add the remaining tablespoon of oil on medium heat to griddle the dumplings.
5. Whenever the oil is glinting, add the dumplings and pan-fry until golden brown on the bottom.
6. In a small cup, mix soy sauce, sesame oil, mustard, and spring onion. Serve warm with dumplings.

2.2 Shredded Chicken Salad with Gochujang Dressing

Cooking Time: 30 minutes
Serving Size: 4
Ingredients:
For the Salad
- ¼ English cucumber
- ¼ small red onion
- ½ bunch watercress
- 3 ounces leaf lettuce
- 2 cups water
- 1 tablespoon table salt
- 1 whole chicken breast half
- 1 cup sake
- 3 slices of ginger

For the Dressing
- 4 teaspoons gochujang
- 2 teaspoons rice vinegar
- 2 tablespoons mirin
- 2 tablespoons sesame oil

Method:
1. Combine the salad ingredients and add seasonings.
2. Mix dressings with salad ingredients. Mix thoroughly and serve.

2.3 Sichuan-Style Braised Eggplant with Pickled Chilies and Garlic

Cooking Time: 30 minutes
Serving Size: 4
Ingredients:
- 2 tablespoons Sichuan chili
- Roughly cilantro leaves
- 4 medium garlic
- 4 scallions
- Kosher salt
- 1 ½ pounds Chinese eggplants
- 3 tablespoons vegetable oil
- 4 teaspoons minced fresh ginger
- 2 red Thai bird chilies
- 1 tablespoon Chinkiang vinegar
- 1 ¼ teaspoons cornstarch
- 3 tablespoons white vinegar
- 1 tablespoon sugar
- 2 teaspoons soy sauce

- 2 tablespoons Shaoxing wine

Method:
1. In a medium mixing bowl, combine ½ cup kosher salt and 2 quarts of water.
2. Toss in the eggplant slices.
3. In the meantime, in a medium bowl, heat white vinegar until it begins to boil.
4. In a small cup, place cut chilies and pour boiling vinegar over them.
5. After that, combine the wine, sugar, sesame oil, and Chinkiang vinegar in a mixing bowl.
6. Cautiously drain the eggplant and allow it to dry with paper towels.
7. In a skillet, heat the oil over high heat until it begins to smoke.
8. Cook with the eggplant. Toss to the sides of the wok.
9. Add the ginger, garlic, and green onions to the wok and return it to high heat.
10. Cook the broad bean paste. Add the chili sauce.
11. Mix thoroughly in a serving bowl, garnish with chopped fresh, dried basil.

2.4 Hot and Numbing Xi'an Style Oven-Fried Chicken Wings

Cooking Time: 1 hour

Serving Size: 4

Ingredients:

- ½ cup cilantro leaves
- 4 scallions
- 1 tablespoon brown sugar
- 2 teaspoons vegetable oil
- 4 pounds chicken wings
- 1 tablespoon red pepper flakes
- 1 tablespoon Sichuan peppercorns
- 1 tablespoon baking powder
- 1 tablespoon whole cumin seed
- 1 teaspoon whole fennel seed
- 1 ½ tablespoon kosher salt

Method:

1. Use paper towels, gently dry the chicken wings.
2. Toss one teaspoon rice flour and one teaspoon salt in a wide mixing bowl until completely and uniformly coated.
3. Place the baking sheet with the wings in the refrigerator for at least 8 hours, covered.
4. Preheat the oven to 450 degrees Fahrenheit.
5. Cook for 20 minutes after adding the chicken wings.
6. In a cup, combine ground spices and flavorings.
7. Move the wings to a big mixing bowl and toss with oil until they are finished.
8. Half of the spice powder and all of the coriander and green onions should be added.
9. Taste one wing and season with more spice powder as required. Serve right away.

2.5 Chinese Bean Curd Rolls Stuffed With Pork, Ginger and Mushroom

Cooking Time: 1 hour
Serving Size: 4
Ingredients:
For the Rolls

- 3 ½ ounces enoki mushrooms
- 1 small carrot
- 3 teaspoons vegetable oil
- 6 sheets bean-curd skin
- 1-ounce shiitake mushroom
- 1 teaspoon sugar
- 1 teaspoon cornstarch
- 1 teaspoon soy sauce

For the Pork Filling

- ½ teaspoon kosher salt
- ½ teaspoon sugar
- 1 teaspoon Shaoxing wine
- ½ teaspoon fresh ginger
- ½ pound ground pork
- 1 teaspoon minced garlic
- 1 teaspoon soy sauce
- ¼ ounce wood ear mushrooms
- 1 ½ teaspoons cornstarch
- 2 teaspoons sesame oil

For the Sauce

- 1 teaspoon sesame oil
- 2 scallions
- 2 teaspoons cornstarch
- ¼ cup water
- 1 cup chicken stock
- ½ teaspoon minced garlic
- ½ teaspoon sugar

- 1 teaspoon Shaoxing wine
- 1 teaspoon oyster sauce
- 1 teaspoon soy sauce

Method:
1. Combine all of the components in a big mixing bowl and stir well.
2. Put it in the fridge for at least 30 minutes, or up to 24 hours.
3. Combine the shiitake mushrooms, sesame oil, sugar, cornflour, and one teaspoon of oil in a mixing bowl. Refrigerate until ready to use.
4. Use two heaping tablespoons of meat filling, make a sandwich.
5. Organize the vegetable and mushroom fillings in a nice pattern.
6. Pull the bean curd skin texture to edge over the liquid.
7. Roll the bean curd covering tightly toward you and shape a neat roll.
8. Heat the remaining two teaspoons of oil in a small saucepan.
9. Make bean-curd rolls in the oven. Place on a plate and set aside to cool for five minutes.
10. Stir together the sauce ingredients and cook until it thickens.
11. Make a steamer. Toss the bean curd rolls in the sauce.
12. Serve the remaining green onion on top of the rolls.

2.6 Crystal Skin Shrimp Dumplings

Cooking Time: 1 hour

Serving Size: 24 dumplings

Ingredients:

For the Dough

- ⅛ teaspoon salt
- 2 teaspoons vegetable oil
- 6 tablespoon tapioca flour
- ¾ cup wheat starch
- ½ cup water

For the Shrimp Filling

- 1 teaspoon cornstarch
- Black vinegar for serving
- ¼ teaspoon white pepper
- 1 teaspoon oil
- ¼ teaspoon salt
- ¼ teaspoon sugar
- ½ pound shrimp
- ½ teaspoon minced garlic
- ½ teaspoon Shaoxing wine
- 1 teaspoon baking soda
- ½ teaspoon minced ginger
- 1 pork fatback

Method:

1. ½ cup of water should be brought to a boil.
2. Combine wheat starch, tapioca cornstarch, and salt in a mixing dish.
3. Combine the flour mixture in a mixing bowl.
4. Combine the oil and the warm water in a mixing bowl.
5. Mix until a loose dough forms with a spatula.
6. Wrap shrimp in cold water and add white vinegar to a medium mixing bowl.
7. Put it in the fridge for 30 minutes before serving.

8. Place the shrimp in a bowl, cut into four to five sections.
9. Salt, sugar, grounded white pepper, oil, and corn flour are combined with minced fatback, diced ginger, garlic powder, Shaoxing wine, seasoning, sugar, ground black pepper, oil, and rice flour.
10. Combine all of the ingredients in a large mixing bowl and set them aside in the fridge.
11. Cut the dough into twelve parts, each weighing around ¼ ounce.
12. Wrap the bags in plastic wrap before you are ready to fill them.
13. To assemble the wrappers, position three to four pieces of seafood in each wrapper's center, along with the fatback.
14. Sear the edge with a small fork.
15. Set up a wok to prepare the dumplings.
16. Every batch of dumplings should be steamed for 7 minutes over medium temperature.
17. Allow five minutes for the dumplings to rest before serving with black vinegar.

2.7 Ground Pork and Corn Congee

Cooking Time: 1 hour and 30 minutes
Serving Size: 4
Ingredients:
- ½ cup short grain rice
- About 1 cup corn
- 2 scallions, chopped
- 6 cups water
- ½ pound ground pork
- 1 ½ teaspoons cornstarch
- 2 teaspoons vegetable oil

- ½ teaspoon minced fresh ginger
- ¼ teaspoon sugar
- ½ teaspoon soy sauce
- ½ teaspoon minced garlic
- Kosher salt
- 1 teaspoon Shaoxing wine

Method:

1. Add meat, spice, cloves, and Shaoxing wine, ¼ teaspoon of salt, sugar, sesame oil, cornstarch, and oil in a mixing bowl.
2. Combine all of the ingredients in a large mixing bowl and set them aside in the fridge.
3. Fill a big pot halfway with water and add the cleaned rice. Make sure the rice is not stuck to the bottom by stirring it.
4. Thirty minutes after the first swirl, cover the pot and then stir the rice once more.
5. Cover the pot once more and cook for another thirty minutes.
6. When the congee is finished, it should have a smooth, silky texture.
7. Boil for ten minutes after adding the ground pork to the congee and bringing it down.
8. Turn the heat down, add the corn, and spice the congee with salt and pepper to taste. Mix thoroughly with green onion sliced on top.

Chapter 3: Chinese Breakfast Recipes

3.1 Vegetable and Noodle Omelets

Cooking Time: 10 minutes
Serving Size: 4

Ingredients:

- 2 teaspoons sesame oil
- 1 tablespoon soy sauce
- 800g packet stir-fry vegetable
- 1 tablespoon oyster sauce
- 2 garlic cloves
- 2cm piece fresh ginger
- 100g rice vermicelli noodles
- 2 green onions
- 1 ½ tablespoon vegetable oil
- 8 eggs

Method:

1. In a heatproof pan, position the noodles.
2. Fill the pot halfway with boiling water.
3. Wait for 3 - 4 minutes, or until the vegetables are soft.
4. Drain the water. In a mixing bowl, whisk together the eggs and onions.
5. In a slow cooker, heat two teaspoons peanut oil over medium temperature.
6. To coat, swirl it around. Garlic and ginger should be added now.
7. Combine the vegetable mixture, oyster sauce, and soy sauce in a mixing bowl. Place it in a mixing bowl.

8. In a 20cm nonstick roasting tray, heat one teaspoon of the residual vegetable oil over medium-high heat.
9. One-quarter of the beaten egg should be added.
10. Heat for 30 seconds, or until the sauce is barely set.
11. One-quarter of the vegetable mixture should be placed on one-half of the omelets.
12. Cook for 1 minute, or until the egg is fully set.
13. To stay warm, cover. To make four omelets, repeat with the remaining oil, beaten eggs, and vegetable combination.

3.2 No-cook Chicken Banh mi

Cooking Time: 15 minutes
Serving Size: 4
Ingredients:
- 1 tablespoon sriracha or chili sauce
- 8 long coriander sprigs
- ½ Coles hot roast chicken
- 200g packet Coles beetroot slaw
- ½ cup whole-egg mayonnaise
- 4 Coles Vietnamese rolls

Method:
1. After cutting all the way across, break each bread wrap in half.
2. Mayonnaise should be spread on the cut ends.
3. Fill with beetroot pesto and meat.
4. If needed, sprinkle with chili sauce.
5. Serve with sprigs of cilantro.

3.3 Scrambled Egg Curry with Tomato Salsa

Cooking Time: 20 minutes
Serving Size: 2

Ingredients:

- Mango chutney
- Chapatti bread
- 8 eggs
- Low-fat Greek yogurt
- 200g grape tomatoes
- ½ teaspoon garam masala
- ¼ teaspoon turmeric
- 12 fresh curry leaves
- 1 small brown onion
- 1 ½ tablespoon grapeseed oil
- ½ cup coriander leaves
- ¾ teaspoon cumin seeds
- ½ teaspoon mustard seeds
- 1 tablespoon lemon juice
- 3 garlic cloves

Method:
1. In a heatproof cup, position the tomato.
2. In a wide nonstick roasting tray, heat two teaspoons of the oils over moderate flame. One garlic clove and bay leaves should be added at this stage.
3. Heat for 1 minute, or until the aromas are released.
4. Pour over the tomato as soon as possible.
5. In the same pan, heat the remaining oil over moderate flame.
6. For two minutes, or until fragrant, stir in cumin seeds.

7. Add the onion and cook for three minutes, or until tender.
8. Stir in the additional garlic and chili for 1 minute, or until fragrant.
9. For two minutes, or until aromatic, stir in the spice and fenugreek.
10.   Pour the egg into the pan—Cook for thirty seconds without stirring.
11.   Serve with salsa verde, yogurt, sorbet, and chapatti on the side.

3.4 Asian Prawn Omelets

Cooking Time: 30 minutes
Serving Size: 4
Ingredients:
- 2 long red chilies
- 1 cup coriander leaves
- 1 large carrot
- 2 spring onions
- 8 eggs
- 24 green king prawns
- 1 red onion
- 3 teaspoons fish sauce
- 80ml peanut oil
- 80g butter

Dressing
- 1 tablespoon caster sugar
- 1 long red chili, seeded
- 2 limes
- 1 tablespoon fish sauce
- 2 cloves garlic

Method:
1. To make the dressing, whisk together all of the components in a small mixing bowl until well mixed.
2. To make omelets, whisk together eggs, shrimp paste, and two tablespoons of cold water in a mixing bowl.
3. In a deep fryer, heat one tablespoon oil and 20g fat over medium–high heat. Cook, sometimes flipping, with six shrimp and a quarter of the onions.
4. One-quarter of the egg mix should be added. Add salt and pepper to taste.
5. To keep the omelets soft, transfer them to a plate and coat them loosely with tape.
6. Toss the vegetables, green onions, bell peppers, and coriander with half of the dressing in a large mixing bowl.
7. Serve the omelets on plates with the salad combination on top.
8. To eat, drizzle with the leftover dressing.

3.5 Banh Xeo (Crispy Pancakes)

Cooking Time: 30 minutes
Serving Size: 8
Ingredients:
- Butter lettuce leaves
- Fresh mint leaves
- 220g rice flour
- 12 cooked prawns
- 130g bean sprouts
- 1 brown onion

- 300g Pork Porterhouse Steak
- 2 tablespoons cornflour
- Pinch of white pepper
- 2 tablespoons peanut oil
- 1 can coconut milk
- 1 teaspoon sugar
- ½ teaspoon salt
- 1 teaspoon ground turmeric
- 310ml iced water

Nuoc Cham
- 1 long fresh red chili
- 1 garlic clove
- 1 ½ tablespoons water
- 1 tablespoon caster sugar
- 60ml fresh lime juice
- 60ml fish sauce

Method:
1. In a small cup, mix the fish sauce, lemon juice, water, butter, chili, and garlic. Mix until the sugar is fully dissolved.
2. In a medium mixing bowl, add flour mixture, coconut milk, water, turmeric, sugar, and salt.
3. Cover and chill for 1 hour or overnight to allow flavors to meld.
4. Preheat a nonstick deep fryer with a 20cm diameter over high heat.
5. Heat 1 tablespoon of oil until it just starts to smoke.
6. Three minutes, or until translucent, stir-fry the onion and meat.
7. One-quarter of the remaining oil should be lightly brushed over the pan. One-quarter of the flour mix should be added now.

8. Three minutes in the oven, half the pancake should be filled with one-quarter of the pork combination and one-quarter of the prawns.
9. To seal the envelope, fold it over. Cover with foil and move to a tray.
10.   Serve with lettuce on the side.

3.6 Peking Chicken Crepes with Snow Pea Salad

Cooking Time: 20 minutes
Serving Size: 4
Ingredients:
- 400g packet French-style crepes
- 8 garlic chives
- 3 cups cooked chicken
- 2/3 cup hoisin sauce
- 150g snow peas
- 50g snow pea sprouts
- 2 Lebanese cucumbers
- 4 green onions

Method:
1. Snow peas should be finely shredded, and onions should be thinly sliced.
2. Place in a mixing bowl. Toss in the cucumber and sprouts.
3. Toss all together. Separate the chicken and the hoisin sauce into two containers.
4. Crepes should be heated according to the instructions on the package.

5. On a tray, place one crepe. One-eighth of the snow pea combination, chicken, and hoisin sauce should be on top.
6. Using a chive, secure the chive.
7. Replace the crepes, snow pea combination, and hoisin sauce with the leftover crepes, snow pea combination, and hoisin sauce. Serve the food.

3.7 Chicken Ginger Congee

Cooking Time: 1 hour 10 minutes
Serving Size: 4
Ingredients:
- 2 teaspoons fried garlic
- Soy sauce to serve
- ½ teaspoon sesame oil
- 1 tablespoon fried shallots
- Salt and ground white pepper
- 2 tablespoons green onion
- 1-liter chicken liquid stock
- 200g chicken tenderloin
- 1 teaspoon Chinese rice wine
- 500ml water
- ½ cup long grain rice
- 4 slices of young ginger

Method:
1. In a wide heavy-based frying pan, carry the chicken broth, water, and spice to a boil over medium temperature.
2. Reduce heat to medium-low and add the garlic.

3. Cook, wrapped, for 1 hour, just until the rice has browned and most of the water has been drained, stirring regularly to prevent the rice from sticking.
4. Simmer for 4-5 minutes, just until the meat is just cooked, after adding the meat to the congee.
5. Dress the congee with salt and pepper after adding the rice wine.
6. Spray the spring onions on top of the congee, sprinkled with sesame oil, and finish with the caramelized onion and garlic.
7. Serve with a side of soy sauce.

3.8 Kimchi Fried Rice with Bacon and Eggs

Cooking Time: 15 minutes
Serving Size: 4
Ingredients:
- 30g unsalted butter
- Thinly sliced garlic chives
- 2 teaspoon sesame oil
- 2 teaspoon soy sauce
- 1 tablespoon rice bran oil
- 4 cups white rice
- 4 eggs
- 1 small onion
- 1 cup kimchi
- 2 tablespoon kimchi juice
- 4 bacon rashers
- 2 garlic cloves
- 1 cup fresh peas
- 1 tablespoon ginger

Method:

1. In a skillet, heat the rice bran oil over moderate flame.
2. For 3-4 minutes, cook, medium heat, or till onions are soft and bacon is crispy.
3. Cook for thirty minutes, after adding the ginger and garlic.
4. Cook by constantly stirring, for two minutes, until peas, sushi, and riceare well cooked. Remove from the heat.
5. In a frying pan, heat the oil over medium-high heat. 2 shells, carefully broken into oil and fried until finished. Remove using a slotted spoon.
6. Return the wok to a moderate heat area.
7. Stir in the soy sauce, sesame oil, butter, and preserved kimchi juices to warm it up.
8. To serve, divide the rice between bowls and top with a poached egg and garlic thyme.

3.9 Chinese Fried Eggs with Sticky Ginger Rice

Cooking Time: 20 minutes
Serving Size: 4
Ingredients:
- 1 long fresh red chili
- Steamed Asian greens
- 2 ½ tablespoons oyster sauce
- 2 green shallots
- 1 tablespoon grapeseed oil
- Grapeseed oil
- 4 eggs
- 1 ½ tablespoons fresh ginger
- 500ml water
- 1 chicken stock cube

- 250g jasmine rice
- 1 garlic clove

Method:
1. In a frying pan, heat the oil over moderate flame.
2. Combine the ginger and garlic in a bowl.
3. Add the rice and mix well.
4. Fill the pot halfway with water and add the stock cube.
5. Get the water to a boil. Lessen to low heat and cook for 12 minutes, uncovered, or until rice is soft.
6. Cover and set aside for five minutes. Toss the rice with a fork to fluff it up.
7. In the meantime, fill a big, deep frying pan with enough extra grapeseed oil to come 1.5cm up the rim.
8. Heat over a medium-high heat area. Toss two eggs into the hot oil.
9. Cook for two minutes, or until golden brown, puffy, and the white is just set.
10. Continue with the leftover eggs.
11. Serve the rice with an egg on top of each plate.
12. Drizzle oyster sauce over the top and top with shallots and chili. Serve with boiled greens on the side.

3.10 Sweet and Sour Eggs

Cooking Time: 15 minutes
Serving Size: 6

Ingredients:
- 2 dried bay leaves
- White pepper, to season
- 1 tablespoon brown sugar
- One teaspoon tamarind puree
- 125ml peanut oil
- 1 tablespoon sambal oelek
- 125ml water
- 6 eggs
- 3 garlic cloves
- 1 brown onion

Method:
1. In a skillet, heat the canola oil over moderate flame.
2. Cook for two minutes, or until golden brown, adding one egg at a time.
3. Cook for another thirty seconds on the other hand.
4. Repeat with the remaining egg and move to a dish.
5. In the same wok, add the ginger and garlic.
6. Stir-fry for three minutes or until the onion turns a golden brown shade.
7. Stir in the sambal oelek until all is well combined.
8. Combine the water, sugar, tamarind puree, and star anise in a large mixing bowl. Get the water to a boil.
9. Reduce the heat to a medium-low setting.
10. Cook for three minutes, or until the sauce thickness increases, before adding the eggs.
11. Add salt and white pepper to taste. Place on a plate to cool.

Chapter 4: Chinese Snack Recipes

4.1 Sweet and Spicy Snacks

Cooking Time: 1 hour 30 minutes
Serving Size: 16
Ingredients:
- ½ teaspoon onion powder
- 2 teaspoons salt
- 2-4 tablespoons hot sauce
- ½ teaspoon garlic powder
- 5 cups corn
- ¼ cup Worcestershire sauce
- ⅓ cup honey or maple syrup
- 1 cup unsalted cashews
- ½ cup butter
- 2 cups mini pretzels
- 1 cup peanuts
- 1 cup almonds
- 2 cups bagel chips

Method:
1. Preheat the oven to 250 degrees Fahrenheit.
2. On a big sheet plate, mix the Chex noodles, pretzels, croissant chips, peanuts, oats, and cashew nuts.
3. Add butter, Balsamic vinegar, sugar or golden syrup, sour cream, garlic powder, smoked paprika, and salt in a small saucepan placed over medium heat.
4. Heat until the butter is fully melted and the mixture is completely smooth.

5. Rub over the Chex mixture and stir to ensure that it is evenly covered.
6. Cook for about 1 to 2 hours, mixing every ten minutes or so, till the snack mix is crispy and fluffy.
7. Allow cooling fully before serving. For several months, store in an airtight bag.

4.2 One-Bowl Caramel Snack Cake

Cooking Time: 60 minutes
Serving Size: 9
Ingredients:
- 1 teaspoon vanilla extract
- Flaky sea salt
- ¾ teaspoon salt
- ¼ cup confectioners' sugar
- 1 ½ teaspoons baking powder
- ¼ teaspoon baking soda
- Cooking oil spray
- 1 cup all-purpose flour
- ¾ cup cake flour
- 2 large egg yolks
- 1 cup heavy cream
- ¾ cup unsalted butter
- 1 tablespoon vanilla extract
- 1 large egg
- 1/3 cup heavy cream
- 1 teaspoon flaky sea salt
- 1 cup dark brown sugar
- 1 cup dark brown sugar

Method:
1. Preheat the oven to 350 degrees Fahrenheit.
2. Use cooking oil mist, spray an 8-inch square plate.
3. Microwave on high for 1 minute, or until butter is melted.
4. Set aside half a cup of the mixture in a big mixing bowl.
5. To the leftover ¼ cup melted butter, add milk and then cinnamon.
6. Mix the sugar, cinnamon, and preserved melted butter in a blending bowl until smooth.
7. Pour in the milk and the caramel sauce.
8. Place the flour mixture into the wet using the sheet.
9. Preheat the oven to 350°F and bake the cake for 20 minutes on the middle rack.
10.   Caramel toppings are added, then slices are split and served.

4.3 Chinese Style Braised

Cooking Time: 2 hours
Serving Size: 6
   Ingredients:
- Steamed bok choy
- Steamed basmati rice
- 3 tablespoon dark soy sauce
- 500ml beef stock
- 3-4 tablespoon olive oil
- 2 teaspoon light sugar
- 3 tablespoon Chinese cooking wine
- 6 garlic cloves
- 1 teaspoon Chinese five-spice powder

- 2-star anise
- Thumb-size root ginger
- 1 ½kg braising beef
- 2 tablespoon plain flour
- 1 red chili
- 1 bunch spring onions

Method:
1. In a big, deep casserole, heat two tablespoons of the oil.
2. Cook the garlic, onions, peppers, and chili in a skillet.
3. Toss the meat in flour, then apply one tablespoon of further oil to the pan and brown in batches.
4. Toss in the five-spice and star anise, then the gingery mixture.
5. Preheat the oven to 150 degrees Celsius.
6. Put in the soy and storage, bring to a boil, then cover loosely and cook in the oven.
7. Add more soy sauce to taste.
8. Place the cooked Bok choy in the bowl, then immediately carry to the table with the brown rice and eat.

4.4 Chinese Meat Filled Buns

Cooking Time: 2 hours 40 minutes
Serving Size: 24 buns
Ingredients:
- 2 ½ tablespoons water
- One recipe Chinese steamed buns
- 1 tablespoon white sugar
- Ground black pepper to taste

- 8 ounces chopped pork
- 1 tablespoon rice wine
- 1 tablespoon vegetable oil
- 1 (4 ounces) can of shrimp
- 1 tablespoon fresh ginger root
- 1 tablespoon light soy sauce
- 2 green onions
- 1 teaspoon salt

Method:
1. In a skillet, cook minced pork over medium-high heat.
2. Set aside to cool after draining and seasoning with salt.
3. Green onions, pepper, sesame oil, white wine, oil, salt, and pepper should be combined.
4. Mix in the minced beef. Add the water and completely mix it in.
5. Preheat the oven to 350°F and prepare the dough for Chinese steamed buns.
6. Form dough balls and tie them around the filling.
7. In a skillet, bring the water to a boil and then reduce the heat to low.
8. Place as many buns on parchment paper as possible.
9. Then use a lid, cover the wok.
10. Heat buns for 20 to 30 minutes over hot water.
11. Steam the buns in groups until they are all finished.

4.5 Chinese Chicken and Mushroom

Cooking Time: 31 minutes
Serving Size: 4

Ingredients:
For the Stir Fry

- 2 green onions
- 1 tablespoon oil
- 2½ cups sliced mushrooms
- 1 clove garlic
- 1 ½ tablespoon bicarb of soda
- 1 lb. chicken breasts

For the Sauce

- ½ teaspoon pepper
- 1 teaspoon sugar
- 1 teaspoon oyster sauce
- 2 teaspoon sesame oil
- 2 tablespoon Chinese cooking wine
- 2 tablespoon soy sauce
- 3 tablespoon cornstarch
- ¾ cup cold chicken stock

Method:

1. Around the grain, cut the meat into small slices.
2. Spray the baking soda over the meat in a mixing bowl and slowly pour to cover.
3. Wash the meat many times to remove the baking soda.
4. In a big glass container, combine all of the sauce components.
5. Put the oil in a heavy-bottomed frying pan over medium temperature.
6. Stir in the spring onions with the bell peppers in the oil.

7. Cook for 2 minutes after adding the chicken to the bowl.
8. Add the remaining mushrooms to the mix.
9. Add the garlic slices.
10. Allow the sauce a final swirl before pouring it into the pan.
11. Serve right away.

4.6 Chinese Pork Belly Buns

Cooking Time: 2 hours 30 minutes
Serving Size: 10 buns

Ingredients:

Steamed Buns

- 3 tablespoon unsalted butter
- 1 tablespoon olive oil
- 2 teaspoon instant dried yeast
- 3 tablespoon whole milk
- 3 ¾ cups flour
- ½ teaspoon salt
- ¾ cup warm water
- 2 tablespoon caster sugar

Slow-Cooked Pork Belly

- 1 tablespoon rice wine
- 1 tablespoon caster sugar
- 1 tablespoon minced ginger
- 3 cloves garlic
- 4 ¼ cups chicken stock
- 2.2 lb. rindless pork belly

Pork Belly Glaze

- 3 tablespoon dark soy sauce
- 1 teaspoon lemongrass paste
- 2 tablespoon honey

- 2 tablespoon brown sugar
- 2 tablespoon vegetable oil
- 1 tablespoon minced ginger
- 1 red chili
- 1 pinch of salt and pepper

Method:
1. Begin by preparing the bao buns.
2. In a mixing bowl, combine the flour, salt, sugar, and yeast.
3. In a jug, combine the milk, hot water, and butter and whisk until the butter has melted.
4. In an oiled pan, position the dough.
5. Begin preparing the pork belly in the meantime.
6. In a pan, combine all of the ingredients for the slow-cooked pork belly.
7. Re-knead the dough and divide it into ten balls.
8. Position the buns on the baking trays in the oven.
9. Place a large wok pan over high heat and bring to a boil.
10. Slice the pork into small bite-size pieces.
11. In a deep fryer, heat one tablespoon of the oil.
12. Add the oil and insert the pork, along with the salt and black pepper, to fry at medium temperature until the pork begins to turn golden.
13. Cover the buns and fill them with a sticky pork belly once they have finished cooking. Sesame seeds should be sprinkled on top.

Chapter 5: Chinese Lunch Recipes

5.1 Skinny Beef and Broccoli Noodles

Cooking Time: 10 minutes
Serving Size: 4

Ingredients:
- 400g pack beef stir-fry strips
- Sliced spring onion
- 1 head broccoli
- 1 tablespoon sesame oil
- 3 blocks egg noodles

For the Sauce
- 1 thumb-sized knob ginger
- 1 tablespoon white wine vinegar
- 1 tablespoon tomato ketchup
- 2 garlic cloves
- 2 tablespoon oyster sauce
- 3 tablespoon low-salt soy sauce

Method:
1. Begin by preparing the sauce.
2. In a small mixing bowl, combine all of the components.
3. Follow the package directions for boiling the noodles.
4. Add broccoli a moment before they are finished.
5. In the meantime, heat the oil in a skillet until very warm, then stir-fry the meat until well golden brown, around 2-3 minutes.
6. Pour in the sauce, give it a good stir, and leave it to simmer for a few minutes before turning off the gas.

7. Drain the noodles, toss them with the beef, and serve immediately, garnished with green onions.

5.2 Asian Steak Roll-Ups

Cooking Time: 35 minutes
Serving Size: 8
Ingredients:
- Kosher salt and black pepper to taste
- Sesame seeds for garnish
- 2 tablespoons olive oil
- Asian glaze
- 4 pounds steak top round
- 1 pound asparagus
- 1 red onion
- 2 large color bell peppers

Method:
1. Preheat oven to 400 degrees Fahrenheit.
2. On a work surface, lay down a few meat strips.
3. Fill each roll with a few slices of onions, peppers, and asparagus.
4. Dress the meat and veggies with salt and pepper to taste.
5. In a medium saucepan, heat the oil over medium-high heat.
6. Caramelize the steak wraps on all surfaces until they are browned.
7. Preheat the oven to 350°F and bake the steak rolls for fifteen minutes.
8. Cover with an Asian glaze to keep hot.
9. Remove the meat rolls from the stove after fifteen minutes of cooking.

10.   Return the steak rolls to the oven for a final ten minutes.
11.   Allow five minutes for the rolls to rest.
12.   Serve with sesame seeds on top and additional sauce on the side, if needed.

5.3 Skinny Panda Express Copycat Chow Mein

Cooking Time: 30 minutes
Serving Size: 4
Ingredients:
- 2 celery stalks
- ½ head cabbage
- 1 tablespoon olive oil
- 1 large onion
- 1 lb. rice noodles
- 2 cloves garlic, minced
- 1 teaspoon ginger
- ½ cup soy sauce

Method:
1. Process noodles once al dente in a wide pot of boiling water as per package instructions.
2. Return to the pot after draining.
3. Combine the soy sauce, ginger, and seasoning in a small cup.
4. Heat the oil in a large frying pan.
5. Cook, medium heat, until the onion, celery, and cabbage are tender, about five to six minutes.
6. In a skillet, combine the noodles and soy sauce and mix to combine.

5.4 Beef and Broccoli Stir-Fry

Cooking Time: 25 minutes
Serving Size: 4
Ingredients:
- 2 tablespoons brown sugar
- 1 teaspoon ground ginger
- 1 small onion
- 1/3 cup soy sauce
- 2 tablespoons vegetable oil
- ½ cup water
- 2 tablespoons water
- 3 tablespoons cornstarch
- 4 cups broccoli florets

Method:
1. Merge two tablespoons cornflour, two tablespoons liquid, and garlic salt in a mixing bowl and whisk until smooth.
2. Toss in the meat.
3. Stir-fry meat in 1 tablespoon oil in a pan cooker or skillet over a moderate flame until optimal doneness is reached; cut and stay warm.
4. In the cooking liquid, stir-fry the onion for 4-5 minutes or until softened.
5. Cook for another three minutes, or until the broccoli is soft but still crisp.
6. Replace the beef in the pan.
7. To make the sauce, whisk together the soy sauce, black pepper, spice, and the remaining one tablespoon cornstarch with ½ cup water until smooth; pour into the jar.
8. Serve with toasted pine nuts on top of rice.

5.5 Kung Pao Shrimp

Cooking Time: 25 minutes
Serving Size: 4
Ingredients:
Stir Fry
- 3 green onions
- ¼ cup dry roasted peanuts
- 1 tablespoon ginger
- ½ teaspoon red pepper flakes
- 2 tablespoons vegetable oil
- 1 green bell pepper
- 1 tablespoon garlic
- 1 red bell pepper
- 1 small onion

Marinade
- 1 tablespoon soy sauce
- 2 teaspoons cornstarch
- ¾ pound shrimp

Sauce
- 1 teaspoon sesame oil
- 1 teaspoon cornstarch
- 1 tablespoon dry sherry
- 1 teaspoon brown sugar
- ⅓ cup chicken stock
- 2 tablespoons hoisin sauce
- ¼ cup soy sauce

Method:
1. In a small cup, combine the seafood, soy sauce, and cornflour.
2. Set aside the components for the sauce.
3. In a pan, heat the vegetable oil over a moderate flame.

4. Stir-fry the seafood for 2-3 minutes, or until it turns yellow.
5. If necessary, add additional oil to the pan before adding the onions.
6. Cook for around 2-3 minutes, or until they melt.
7. Add the garlic, ginger, and chili flakes, as well as the red and green bell peppers.
8. Cook for five minutes or until the veggies soften slightly.
9. Cook, constantly stirring, until the sauce thickens.
10. Serve over rice with spring onions and nuts.

5.6 Baked Honey-Garlic Skillet Chicken

Cooking Time: 35 minutes
Serving Size: 4
Ingredients:
- Sesame seeds, for garnish
- Scallions, for garnish
- 1 tablespoon cornstarch
- 1 lb. chicken breasts
- ¼ cup soy sauce
- 1 teaspoon sriracha
- 2 tablespoon sesame oil
- 2 cloves garlic, minced
- Juice of 1 lime
- 3 tablespoon honey

Method:
1. Preheat the oven to 350 degrees Fahrenheit.

2. Spoon combined sesame oil, sugar, garlic, lemon juice, Sriracha, one tablespoon soy sauce, and cornstarch in a medium mixing cup.
3. Season the chicken with salt and black pepper before serving.
4. Heat oil in an oven-safe saucepan over medium heat.
5. Braise the chicken for four minutes until crispy, then turn and cook for another four minutes.
6. Pour the glaze over the top and bake in the oven.
7. Bake for 25 minutes, or until meat is cooked through.
8. Broil for two minutes after sprinkling glaze over chicken.
9. Serve with spring onions and sesame seeds as garnish.

5.7 Ginger Pork Pot Stickers

Cooking Time: 1 hour 35 minutes
Serving Size: 5 dozen
Ingredients:
For Dumplings
- 60 dumpling wrappers
- Vegetable oil
- 1 large egg, lightly beaten
- Flour, for surface
- 2 teaspoon ginger
- 2 teaspoon fish sauce
- 1 lb. ground pork
- 2 tablespoon low-sodium soy sauce
- 2 teaspoon sesame oil
- ¼ cup chicken broth
- 2 cloves garlic

- 2 green onions

For Dipping Sauce
- 3 tablespoon rice wine vinegar
- ¼ cup soy sauce

Method:

1. Mix the pork, stock, white sections of spring onions, ginger, sesame oil, soy sauce, spice, fish sauce if used, and egg in a big mixing bowl.
2. In a large frying pan, heat one tablespoon olive oil over moderate flame.
3. Dumplings should be arranged on an even surface.
4. Fry for 1–2 minutes, or until golden brown on the bottom.
5. Reduce heat to medium-low and protect with a tight-fitting lid after adding 1/3 cup water to the skillet.
6. Cook for another three minutes, or until there is no more water.
7. In a medium mixing cup, whisk together soy sauce, rice wine vinegar, and the reserved green bits of spring onions.
8. Potstickers should be served with a dipping sauce.

5.8 Shrimp Wontons

Cooking Time: 30 minutes
Serving Size: 14 wontons

Ingredients:
- Cooking spray
- 2-4 tablespoon sweet chili sauce
- 1 tablespoon fresh chives

- 14 won-ton wrappers
- Eight large shrimp
- ½ teaspoon red pepper flakes
- ¼ teaspoon salt
- 1 clove garlic
- 2 tablespoon feta cheese
- ½ teaspoon garlic powder
- Three tablespoon cream cheese
- 1 teaspoon butter

Method:
1. Preheat the oven to 400 degrees Fahrenheit.
2. It is entirely up to you if you sauté the seafood in 1 teaspoon of olive oil or butter. Cook with the garlic.
3. Shrimp should be minced into very small bits.
4. Combine the cheeses, chives, red pepper, garlic salt, and spice in a small mixing bowl.
5. Fill each wonton with a heaping teaspoon of the seafood combination.
6. Preheat oven to 400°F and bake for 5-7 minutes until it is lightly browned.
7. Serve hot with a side of sweet chili sauce for dipping!

5.9 Moo Goo Gai Pan

Cooking Time: 40 minutes
Serving Size: 3
Ingredients:
- 1 tablespoon rice wine
- ¼ cup chicken broth
- 1 tablespoon soy sauce

- 1 tablespoon cornstarch
- 1 tablespoon white sugar
- 1 tablespoon oyster sauce
- 2 cloves garlic
- 1 pound chicken breast
- 1 tablespoon vegetable oil
- 15 ounce can straw mushrooms
- 1 tablespoon vegetable oil
- 1 cup fresh mushrooms
- 8-ounce bamboo shoots
- 8-ounce water
- 2 cups broccoli florets

Method:

1. In a griddle or broad skillet, heat one tablespoon olive oil over medium temperature until it starts to smoke.
2. Fresh mushrooms, lettuce, bamboo shoots, artichoke hearts, and straw shiitake should all be added at this stage.
3. Continue cooking for five minutes, or until all the veggies are hot and the lettuce is soft.
4. In the skillet, heat the remaining tablespoon of vegetables until it starts to smoke.
5. Heat for several seconds, constantly stirring, before the garlic turns lightly golden.
6. Toss in the chicken.
7. In a small cup, combine the cornstarch, sugar, sesame oil, oyster sauce, white wine, and chicken broth.
8. Cook for 30 seconds, or until the sauce has thickened.
9. Toss the veggies back into the wok with the sauce.

Chapter 6: Chinese Dinner Recipes

6.1 Chinese Chicken Skewers

Cooking Time: 45 minutes
Serving Size: 4
Ingredients:
Marinade
- 2 cloves garlic
- 1 ½ teaspoon fresh ginger
- 1 teaspoon sesame oil
- 1 teaspoon white sugar
- 3 tablespoon oyster sauce
- 1 tablespoon Chinese cooking wine
- 2 teaspoon sriracha sauce
- 1 tablespoon soy sauce

Skewers
- 12 bamboo skewers
- 2 tablespoon vegetable oil
- 1.5 lb. chicken thighs

Method:
1. In a mixing dish, blend the marinade components.
2. Set aside for at least thirty minutes, or up to midnight, to caramelize the chicken.
3. Use skewers, thread the chicken onto the skewers.
4. In a medium saucepan, heat one tablespoon of oil on a moderate flame.
5. Heat half of the skewers for three to five minutes on each side until it is soft, lightly browned, pressing them down with a spatula to ensure even cooking.

6. Continue with the available skewers.
7. Serve warm with thinly chopped scallions as a garnish.

6.2 Sesame Chinese Chicken with Rice

Cooking Time: 30 minutes
Serving Size: 4
Ingredients:
Sauce
- 2 tablespoon brown sugar
- 4 tablespoon soy sauce
- 2 tablespoon sweet chili sauce
- 3 tablespoon ketchup
- 1 tablespoon sesame oil
- 1 tablespoon Chinese rice vinegar
- 1 tablespoon honey
- 2 cloves garlic

Other Ingredients
- 2 teaspoon paprika
- 3 chicken breast fillets
- ½ teaspoon pepper
- ½ teaspoon garlic salt
- 5 tablespoon vegetable oil
- 10 tablespoon plain flour
- ½ teaspoon salt
- 3 tablespoon cornflour
- 2 eggs

To Serve
- 2 tablespoon sesame seeds
- Small bunch of spring onions
- Boiled rice

Method:
1. In a griddle or big frying pan, add the oil until it is very warm.
2. Put the egg in one small dish and the corn starch in another small bowl while the oil is heating.
3. In a separate shallow dish, combine the rice, salt, pepper, garlic powder, and paprika.
4. Dig the chicken in cornmeal, then in egg, and then in prepared rice.
5. In a hot wok, combine all of the sauce components, stir, and cook over high heat until the sauce has reduced by about a third.
6. Return the chicken to the pan and throw it in the sauce to coat it.
7. Cover with sesame oil and green onions and serve with steamed rice.

6.3 Honey Chicken

Cooking Time: 30 minutes
Serving Size: 6
Ingredients:
- 2 tablespoons rice wine vinegar
- 1 tablespoon soy sauce
- 1/3 cup honey
- ¼ cup water
- 6 chicken thighs
- 2 teaspoons garlic powder
- 6 cloves garlic
- Salt and pepper

Method:

1. Put aside chicken that has been seasoned with salt, pepper, and cayenne pepper.
2. Brine chicken thighs cutlets in a pan or skillet over medium-low heat.
3. Turn off the heat after both sides have been seared, protect the pan with a cover, and continue to cook.
4. Drain the majority of the residual water from the bowl, leaving about two tablespoons to add flavor.
5. Between the meats, add the onion and fry until aromatic.
6. Combine the honey, water, vinegar, and sesame oil in a mixing bowl.
7. Reduce the heat to moderate and simmer until the sauce has thickened and reduced slightly.
8. Serve over tomatoes, rice, pasta, or with a salad garnished with parsley.

6.4 Egg Foo Young

Cooking Time: 20 minutes
Serving Size: 4
Ingredients:
- 2 tablespoons white vinegar
- 2 tablespoons soy sauce
- 2 tablespoons cornstarch
- 2 tablespoons sugar
- 2 tablespoons vegetable oil
- 3 cups chicken broth
- 1 cup cooked small shrimp
- ¼ teaspoon garlic powder
- 4 eggs
- ⅓ cup green onions
- 8 ounces bean sprouts

Method:
1. In a mixing bowl, whisk together the eggs, black beans, spring onions, seafood, and sour cream until thoroughly mixed.
2. To create a patty, heat oil in a saucepan over medium heat and dump about half a cup of the beaten egg into the pan.
3. Repeat with the remaining beaten egg and cook until lightly browned, around three minutes per hand.
4. Remove the patties from the pan and set them aside.
5. In a pan over medium heat, stir together all the chicken stock, cornflour, sugar, mustard, and soy sauce until the liquid thickness increases and simmers, around five minutes.
6. Spread the sauce on top of the patties.

6.5 Chinese BBQ Pork Puns

Cooking Time: 4 hours 25 minutes
Serving Size: 16 buns
Ingredients:
For the Filling
- 2 tablespoons all-purpose flour
- 2 cups Chinese roast pork
- 2 teaspoons dark soy sauce
- ¾ cup chicken stock
- 2 tablespoons vegetable oil
- 2 tablespoons oyster sauce
- 1 ½ teaspoon sesame oil

- ½ cup shallots
- 2 teaspoons light soy sauce
- 2 tablespoons sugar

For the Dough
- One tablespoon active dry yeast
- 1 ½ teaspoons salt
- ½ cup cake flour
- 3 ½ cups bread flour
- 2/3 cup heavy cream
- 1 large egg
- 1/3 cup sugar
- 1 cup milk

To Finish the Buns
- 1 tablespoon sesame seeds
- 1 tablespoon granulated sugar
- Egg wash

Method:
1. Begin with the crème Fraiche, milk, and egg, all of which should be at ambient temperature.
2. Then, add the milk, pastry flour, bread, yeast, and spice within this order.
3. To put the dough around, switch the mixer to the lowest position.
4. Form a ball out of the dough. Protect for 75-90 minutes in a hot environment.
5. Combine the rest of the ingredients with the roasted pork.
6. Transfer the filling from the skillet onto a large plate after turning off the heat.
7. Cut the dough into 16 bits that are all the same size.
8. Roll it into a 4-inch disc, significant in the middle than the corners.

9. Cover the bun with 1 part of the filling.

10.   Preheat oven to 350°F and bake for 22-25 minutes until it is lightly browned.

6.6   Baked   Sweet   and   Sour   Chicken, Pineapple, Carrots, and Bell Peppers

Cooking Time: 50 minutes
Serving Size: 6

Ingredients:
Sweet and Sour Sauce
- ½ teaspoon red pepper flakes
- ½ teaspoon ginger powder
- 4 garlic cloves
- 1 teaspoon salt
- ½ cup pineapple juice
- 1 small onion
- 2 tablespoons soy sauce
- 1 ½ cups sugar
- ¼ cup ketchup
- 1 cup red wine vinegar

Chicken Breading
- ¼ teaspoon ginger powder
- ¼ teaspoon onion powder
- ½ teaspoon salt
- ¼ teaspoon pepper
- 3-4 chicken breasts
- 1 1/3 cup cornstarch
- ½ teaspoon garlic powder
- ½ cup flour
- 3 eggs

Vegetables
- 1 red bell pepper

- 1 cup carrots sliced
- 1 green bell pepper
- 1-20 oz. can pineapple

Method:
1. In a small saucepan, combine the components for the "Sweet and Sour Sauce," mix to combine, bring to the boil, then decrease to a gentle simmer.
2. Preheat the oven to 350 degrees Fahrenheit.
3. In a big mixing bowl, mix the eggs and set them aside.
4. In a small cup, whisk together the cornflour, garlic salt, salt, pepper, spice powder, and smoked paprika; set aside beside flour.
5. Combine the chicken and the eggs.
6. Move the meat in the bag in the freezer to uniformly coat it in cornstarch.
7. Cook for 1-2 minutes per pound of chicken.
8. Toss in the carrots, mango, and pepper with the sweetness and spice until everything is well mixed.
9. Cook, stirring regularly, for half an hour, or until sauce thickness increases.

6.7 Chinese cabbage Stir-Fry

Cooking Time: 15 minutes
Serving Size: 4
Ingredients:
- 1 tablespoon soy sauce
- 1 tablespoon Chinese cooking wine
- 2 cloves garlic, minced

- 1 pound shredded cabbage
- 1 tablespoon vegetable oil

Method:
1. In a slow cooker or big skillet, steam the vegetable oil over medium-high heat.
2. Add ginger and garlic.
3. Heat for a few moments, constantly stirring, before the garlic starts to brown.
4. Wrap the skillet and cook over medium heat after stirring in the cabbage until it is fully coated in oil.
5. Continue cooking for another minute after adding the soy sauce.
6. Mix in the Chinese cooking wine and raise the heat to be large.
7. Cook and stir for another two minutes, just until the cabbage is soft.

6.8 Grilled Chinese Char Siu Chicken

Cooking Time: 65 minutes
Serving Size: 4
Ingredients:
- Scant two teaspoons sesame oil
- 1 ¾ pounds chicken thighs
- 1 ½ tablespoons soy sauce
- 1 tablespoon ketchup
- 1 large garlic clove
- 2 tablespoons honey
- 2 tablespoons hoisin sauce
- ¼ teaspoon Chinese five-spice powder

Method:

1. Combine the garlic, five-spice mixture, butter, hoisin, sesame oil, tomato soup, and cardamom oil in a large mixing bowl.
2. Three tablespoons of the sauce should be put down for glazing the meat.
3. Add the meat to the bowl and cover it thoroughly.
4. Cover with cling film and leave to marinate to room temperature for 30 minutes.
5. Set a cast-iron kettle grill skillet over medium heat and gently oil it.
6. Cook for 7 to 9 minutes, rotating the meat many times.
7. Organize a large charcoal fire or heat it a gas grill to high and cook chicken for 8 to 10 minutes, basting every 3 minutes.
8. Before serving, move to a platter and set aside for ten minutes.

Chapter 7: Chinese Desserts Recipes

7.1 Almond Jelly

Cooking Time: 3 hours 10 minutes
Serving Size: 6
Ingredients:
- ¾ cup sugar
- 1 ½ teaspoons almond extract
- 1 cup water
- 2 cups milk
- 2 (.25 ounce) gelatin powder
- 1 cup water

Method:
1. In a mixing bowl, add 1 cup water, scatter the gelatin over it, and mix until the gelatin is partly absorbed.
2. Remove from the heat.
3. In a big saucepan, carry 1 cup mixture to a boil.
4. Reduce heat to moderate and add the gelatin solution gradually.
5. Pour the milk, sugars, and almond extracts into a wide, shallow container and mix until the glucose and gelatin are dissolved completely.
6. Put it in the fridge for 3 to 4 hours, or until strong.
7. To eat, cut into small pieces.

7.2 Red Bean Popsicles

Cooking Time: 35 minutes
Serving Size: 6
Ingredients:
- 25g caster sugar
- 100g sweet red bean paste
- 125ml cream
- 2 egg yolks
- 250ml milk

Method:
1. In a small saucepan, carry the milk and butter to a low boil.
2. Remove the pan from the heat and set it aside.
3. In a mixing bowl, whisk together two egg yolks and sugars till the combination is light and moist.
4. Mix in the sweet red condensed milk with the glucose and yolk combination.
5. Load the warm wet ingredients into the beaten egg in a steady stream, constantly whisking until smooth.
6. Spoon the sauce into a large casserole dish and cook for five minutes on low heat, stirring constantly.
7. Freeze it in the refrigerator.
8. Fill an ice cream maker halfway with the chilled combination.
9. For about twenty minutes, run the ice cream machine.

7.3 Fa Gao

Cooking Time: 20 minutes
Serving Size: 10 cakes
Ingredients:
- ¼ cup rice flour
- 1 tablespoon baking powder
- ¼ cup neutral oil
- 1 ¼ cups all-purpose flour
- ½ cup dark brown sugar

Method:
1. Position a 10-inch wooden or steel steamer bucket in a 12-inch pan or skillet filled with around 2 inches of water.
2. In a food processor or blender, whisk together the brown sugar, oil, and ¾ cup warm water until the sugar is dissolved, around 1 minute.
3. Scroll the all-purpose flour and corn starch into the sugar syrup in three batches, stirring between each inclusion until no dry spots remain.
4. Fill the egg tart molds to the tip.
5. Under medium temperature, bring water in the pan to a gentle simmer.
6. Place the molds on a cooling rack to clear.
7. Repeat the bubbling process with the remaining five molds in the steamer basket.
8. Hot or at ambient temperature, prepare the cakes.

7.4 Pineapple Buns

Cooking Time: 2 hours 42 minutes
Serving Size: 12 buns
Ingredients:
For the Topping Dough
- 1 egg yolk
- ⅛ teaspoon vanilla extract
- ¼ cup vegetable shortening
- 2 tablespoons milk
- ¼ cup nonfat dry milk powder
- ¼ teaspoon baking powder
- 2/3 cup superfine sugar
- ½ teaspoon baking soda
- 1¼ cups all-purpose flour

For the Bread Dough
- 1 tablespoon active dry yeast
- 1 ½ teaspoons salt
- ½ cup cake flour
- 3 ½ cups bread flour
- 2/3 cup heavy cream
- 1 large egg
- 1/3 cup sugar
- 1 cup milk

To Finish the Buns
- 1 egg yolk

Method:
1. Begin by making the dough for the bread.
2. Combine the dough components in the bucket of an electric mixer.

3. The dough is prepared for proofing after fifteen minutes.
4. Allow the buns to rise for the next hour under a clean, wet kitchen towel.
5. In a measuring dish, add the dry powdered milk.
6. Combine the flour, white vinegar, icing sugar, and superfine sugar in a large mixing bowl.
7. To mix, stir all together.
8. Combine the shortening, butter, egg yolk, and vanilla essence in a mixing bowl.
9. Heat the oven to 350 degrees F once the buns have finished growing a second time.
10. Divide the coating dough into 12 equal portions and roll each into a ball.
11. Rub with egg white and cook for 12-13 minutes at 350 degrees.

7.5 Mung Bean Cake

Cooking Time: 1 hour
Serving Size: 1
Ingredients:
- 110g sugar
- A small pinch of salt
- 40g butter
- 50g vegetable oil
- 250g yellow mung beans
Coloring
- 5-8 g Matcha powder

Method:
1. The yellow mung beans should be pre-soaked overnight.

2. Add enough clean water to cover the mung beans in a medium-slow cooker partially.
3. Cook according to the bean method until the beans are light and easy to break.
4. Then, using a spoon, mash them together until you have a nice and fine blend. Place it in a nonstick skillet.
5. Toss the mung bean combination with a pinch of salt, oil, and cooking oil.
6. Heat over medium-low heat, stirring constantly.
7. When the oil has been fully absorbed, add the sugar.
8. Gradually stir till they can comfortably stick together. Switch the stove off.
9. Then, using a spatula, pass the solution to a filter.
10. If you want to have more, pour the dough into shorter doughs of 30g to 40g and cover ten fillings.
11. Use a mooncake mold or some other mold to shape the mooncakes.
12. This phase should be performed when the combination is warm and not hot.

7.6 Sesame Seed Balls

Cooking Time: 2 hours
Serving Size: 8 balls
   Ingredients:
- ¼ cup sesame seeds
- 4 cups peanut oil
- ¼ cup room temperature water
- 7 ounces lotus paste
- 1 ½ cups glutinous rice flour
- ¼ cup boiling water

- 1/3 cup granulated sugar

Method:
1. To make the sesame ball flour, combine all of the ingredients in a mixing bowl.
2. In a mixing bowl, combine half a cup of glutinous rice sugar and flour.
3. Into the sugar and flour, pour ¼ cup boiling water. ¼ cup ambient temperature water and the remaining glutinous flour are added.
4. The mass of your coating should be half that of your dough ball.
5. Roll the ball in sesame oil that has been soaked until it is fully coated.
6. In a medium deep bowl, heat 4 cups almond or soybean oil to a comfortable 320°F.
7. In a small bowl, toss four sesame balls in the liquid.
8. Fry for the next five minutes, or till they turn a soft golden color, for a maximum of 17-18 minutes.
9. To remove the oil, place the completed sesame balls in a fine-mesh sieve, cooling rack, or sheet lined with towels.
10. Allow cooling for ten minutes before serving.

7.7 Sachima

Cooking Time: 1 hour
Serving Size: 4
Ingredients:
Noodle Dough
- ⅛ teaspoon salt
- ½ teaspoon. baking soda

- 2 large eggs
- 200g all-purpose flour

Syrup
- 60g maltose
- 40 water
- 130g white sugar

Others
- ¼ cup cornstarch for dusting

Method:
1. Combine the all-purpose flour, brown sugar, and spice, and then stir in the egg fluid.
2. Combine all ingredients in a ball and whisk until smooth.
3. Allow the dough to rest for at least thirty minutes after covering it.
4. Heat the oil until it is extremely hot, then measure with one strip.
5. Tiny batches of strips should be fried until they are slightly orange.
6. Shake off any excess oil before placing all of the strips in a big jar.
7. Add sugar, sucrose, salt, and water in a large saucepot.
8. Warm the fluid over a moderate flame until it reaches 115 degrees Celsius.
9. By streams, pour the fluid into the flour. Mix thoroughly, attempting to cover each strip in syrup.
10. Store toppings in airtight bags and store at room temperature for up to 1 week.

Chapter 8: Chinese Soup Recipes

8.1 Simple Chinese Oxtail Soup

Cooking Time: 7 hours 5 minutes
Serving Size: 8
Ingredients:
- Salt
- Chopped cilantro
- 1 large onion
- 1 medium Chinese turnip
- 12 cups water
- 2 ½ pounds oxtails

Method:
1. Heat the oven to 180 degrees Celsius.
2. Clean the oxtails by rinsing them under cold water and patting them dry with a paper towel.
3. Roast for thirty minutes after arranging them on a cookie dish.
4. Add 12 cups of water to a stockpot when the oxtails are frying.
5. Bring to a boil with the vegetables and grilled oxtails.
6. Reduce the heat to a very low boil right away.
7. Cook for around 6 hours, covered, on low heat.
8. Mind to skim off the fat regularly.
9. Add the cabbages for about thirty minutes until you are ready to eat.
10. Simmer until the vegetables are tender, then season with salt and pepper to taste.
11. Serve with green onion on top.

8.2 Lotus Root and Pork Soup

Cooking Time: 7 hours
Serving Size: 12
Ingredients:
- 12 cups cold water
- Salt 1 scallion
- 4 slices ginger
- 1 tablespoon goji berries
- 1 cup re-hydrated seaweed
- 1 pound lotus root
- 2 pounds pork ribs

Method:
1. Rinse the pork ribs or collar bones for an hour in ice water.
2. To caramelize the pork bones, bring a big pot of water to a boil.
3. Remove the pork bones from the fire, rinse, and thoroughly wash them.
4. Simply wash the salmon in a basin of water after it has been soaked until the water is clear.
5. After that, remove it and return it to the pot.
6. First, combine all of the prepared materials in a stockpot, including the pork, lotus root, seaweed, ginger, goji berries, and cold water.
7. Bring it to a boil, then reduce to low heat and keep it there.
8. Allow for at least 4 hours of simmering time.
9. Season with salt and pepper to taste, and finish with chopped green onion.

8.3 Asian Vegetable Stock

Cooking Time: 1-2 hours
Serving Size: 15
  Ingredients:
- ¾ cup coriander
- 6 liters cold water
- 6 celery sticks, sliced
- 10 spring onions
- 1 tablespoon sea salt
- 3 medium carrots
- 1 tablespoon vegetable oil
- 15 slices ginger
- 10 garlic cloves, crushed
- 2 medium red onions

Method:
1. In a cooking pouch, heat the oil, add the onions, garlic, cloves, salt, and cook for one minute over medium temperature.
2. Reduce heat to low and add carrots, fennel, green onions, and cardamom; cook, frequently stirring, for another three minutes or until veggies are nicely browned.
3. Take the water to a boil in the kettle.
4. Remove the stock from the heat and strain it through a muslin cloth.
5. Cool, then keep for up to three days in the fridge or three to four months in the freezer, sealed.

8.4 Ching Po Leung Cantonese Herb Pork Bone Soup

Cooking Time: 5 hours
Serving Size: 8
Ingredients:
- 3 quarts cold water
- Salt
- 2 dried honey dates
- 1 large piece of dried seafood
- 1½ pounds pork bones
- 15 grams Polygonatum datum
- 10 grams dried longan
- 4 slices fresh ginger
- 20 grams fox nut barley
- 10 grams dried goji berries
- 45 grams dried Chinese yam
- 25 grams dried lotus seeds
- 60 grams Chinese pearl barley

Method:
1. Wash the pork ribs for an hour in ice water.
2. Place the pork ribs in a large slow cooker and cover with enough ice water to fully drench them. Increase the heat to high and bring to a boil.
3. Switch off the heat after that. Also, wash the sauté pan.
4. Return the pork bones to the bath, along with the ginger, all of the dried herbs, and three quarts of ice water.
5. Bring it to a boil, then reduce to low heat and keep it there. Allow three hours for the soup to boil.

6. Skim some fat from the top of the soup before eating.
7. Season with salt and pepper, and serve immediately with soy sauce on the side for coating your pork.

8.5 Chinese Watercress Soup with Pork Ribs

Cooking Time: 3 hours 40 minutes
Serving Size: 8
Ingredients:
- White pepper to taste
- Soy sauce to serve
- 1 to 2 bunches of watercress
- 1¼ teaspoon sea salt
- 5 slices ginger
- 8 cups water
- 1½ pounds pork rib tips or ribs

Method:
1. Blanch the bones first. Six cups of water are brought to a boil in a big pot.
2. Toss in the pulled pork. Bring the water down to a boil, then turn off the heat after two minutes.
3. In a fresh pot, combine the blanched roast pork, crushed ginger pieces, and eight glasses of water.
4. Bring the mixture to a boil, then reduce the heat to a low setting.
5. Cover and cook for 90 minutes.
6. During 90 minutes, mix in 1¼ teaspoons of pepper, lock, and boil for another thirty minutes.
7. Mix in the watercress and bring to a boil, covered.
8. Sprinkle with salt and freshly ground black pepper.

9. Serve the broth with a hot cup of porridge and a tiny dish of mild soy sauce as a side dish for the pork.

8.6 Shanghai Style Red Vegetable Soup

Cooking Time: 2 hours 10 minutes
Serving Size: 8
Ingredients:
- 1 teaspoon black pepper
- 1 pound potatoes
- 5 bay leaves
- 2 teaspoons salt
- 2 large carrots
- ¼ cabbage
- 2 pounds oxtails
- 2 tablespoons tomato paste
- 10 cups water
- 2 tablespoons vegetable oil
- 6 cloves garlic
- 3 small tomatoes
- 2 large onions

Method:
1. Take 2 pounds of oxtails, rinse, and thoroughly dry.
2. Cook the oxtails in 2 tablespoons of oil in a dense soup saucepan over medium heat.
3. From both sides, softly brown the oxtails.
4. Break three small tomatoes into hard pieces while the onion is baking.
5. When the vegetables have weakened, add them to the bowl.

6. Turn the heat up to high and put 10 cups of water.
7. Slice the vegetables and broccoli into small pieces and combine them with five basil leaves, two teaspoons salt, and one teaspoon garlic powder in a large pot.
8. Bring to the boil, then drop to low heat and cook for 60 minutes.
9. Extract and cut the potatoes, then return them to the soup after 60 minutes of simmering. When serving, season with salt and pepper to taste.

8.7 Simple Wonton Soup

Cooking Time: 2 hours
Serving Size: 8
Ingredients:
- 6 cups chicken stock
- 1 scallion
- 2 tablespoons Shaoxing wine
- 1 package wonton wrappers
- 10 oz. baby bok choy
- 1 tablespoon soy sauce
- ½ teaspoon salt
- 8 oz. ground pork
- ⅛ teaspoon white pepper
- 2 ½ tablespoons sesame oil

Method:
1. Begin by cleaning the vegetables completely.
2. Bring a big pot of water to a boil and caramelize the vegetables for a few minutes, only before they are wilted.

3. Combine the coarsely diced vegetables, pork belly, and spices in a medium mixing dish.
4. Fill the center with a little more than a teaspoon of the coating.
5. To get a firm seal, divide the wrapper in half and bring the two sides to close.
6. To make the broth, bring your chicken stock to a boil and season with a pinch of salt and white pepper.
7. A different pot of water should be brought to a boil.
8. Continue adding the wontons to the pot a few at a time.
9. Make sure they are not overcooked.
10. Garnish with scallions after pouring the soup over the wontons. Serve it up!

8.8 Chinese Chicken and Mushroom Soup

Cooking Time: 1 hour 30 minutes
Serving Size: 8
Ingredients:
- Salt
- 1 scallion
- 5 slices ginger
- 2 tablespoons Shaoxing wine
- 1 small organic chicken
- 1 tablespoon oil
- 20 small dried shiitake mushrooms
- 2 tablespoons dried goji berries
- 4 dried Chinese dates
- 8 cups water

Method:
1. To begin, simply wash the dried shitake mushrooms a bunch of times.
2. While cooking, remove the stems and return the mushrooms to the pot of boiling water.
3. In a soup pot, combine the preserved goji berries and preserved Chinese dates.
4. Over a high flame, bring to the boil.
5. Shave the chicken thighs and set them aside for another pan.
6. Heat a skillet over medium-low heat until it begins to smoke marginally after the soup has boiled for thirty minutes.
7. To coat the skillet, spread the oil all over it.
8. In a soup pot, add the meat. ½ cup water to pan sear the skillet and add it to the casserole dish as well.
9. Season with salt and freshly chopped scallion just before serving.

Chapter 9: Chinese Salad Recipes

9.1 Mung Bean Clear Noodle Chinese Salad

Cooking Time: 7 minutes
Serving Size: 2
Ingredients:
- Coriander, chopped
- Fresh chili, chopped
- 3 tablespoon spicy black bean sauce
- 1 teaspoon black rice vinegar
- 3½ cup water
- ½ cup mung bean starch

Method:
1. In a mixing bowl, combine ½ cup water and mung bean starch.
2. In a frying pan, heat and cook 3 cups of water until tiny bubbles started to emerge at the bottom.
3. Pour in the flour and water mixture easily with a spoon, stirring continuously.
4. When you see large air bubbles rising to the surface and the liquid appears transparent, remove the pan from the oven.
5. Fill a container halfway with the combination.
6. Allow cooling before refrigerating until it forms a solid paste.
7. Serve with coriander and fresh chili on the side.
8. Black rice is used as a seasoning.

9.2 Pickled Chinese Salad

Cooking Time: 40 minutes
Serving Size: 6
Ingredients:
- A small handful of whole cilantro leaves
- 2 teaspoons white sesame seeds
- 2 large garlic cloves
- Red pepper flakes
- 1 teaspoon kosher salt
- 2 teaspoons soy sauce
- 1 tablespoon grapeseed
- 1 ½ tablespoons rice vinegar
- 2 teaspoons sesame oil
- 2 teaspoons granulated sugar

Method:
1. Cucumbers should be rinsed and dried.
2. Place a cucumber slice cut piece down on a cutting board.
3. Toss the cucumber parts with a large pinch of salt and a large bit of sugar in a colander.
4. Combine the sugar, salt, and rice wine vinegar in a small cup.
5. Stir until the salt and sugar have fully dissolved.
6. Combine the soy sauce and oil in a mixing bowl.
7. When ready to serve, give the cucumbers a good shake to remove any leftover marinade and place them in a serving bowl.
8. Mix thoroughly with cilantro and sesame seeds as a garnish.

9.3 Grilled Mushroom and Chicken Chinese Salad

Cooking Time: 20 minutes
Serving Size: 4
Ingredients:
- 2 teaspoons sugar
- Salt to taste
- 1 ½ tablespoon lemon juice
- 7-8 black peppercorns
- ½ iceberg lettuce
- Olive oil 1 tablespoon
- 300 grams chicken breast
- 1 medium red capsicum
- 6 black olives stoned and sliced
- 6 large button mushrooms
- Oil 2 tablespoons
- 1 yellow capsicum
- Salt to taste
- ½ teaspoon mustard paste
- ½ teaspoon garlic paste
- ½ teaspoon black pepper powder

Method:
1. For twenty minutes, caramelize the chicken thighs in salt, spice paste, mustard powder, and fenugreek seeds.
2. To make the dressing, whisk together all of the components.
3. For five to ten minutes on the grill, cook the chicken breasts.
4. Allow cooling before slicing and setting aside.
5. Roast the mushrooms for two minutes after brushing them with oil.

6. Put aside after cutting into pieces.
7. Grill the red and yellow capsicums for ten minutes, rotating once or twice to ensure even cooking.
8. Remove the seeds, cut in the quarter, pick, and set aside.
9. In a big mixing bowl, combine the chicken, onions, bell peppers, olives, and broccoli.
10.   Toss the salad in the seasoning to combine it. Serve right away.

9.4 Chickpea Chinese Salad

Cooking Time: 40 minutes
Serving Size: 8
Ingredients:
Salad
- 1½ cups small broccoli florets
- ½ cup salted cashews
- 1 cup red bell pepper
- 2 cups red cabbage
- 1 15.5 oz. can chickpeas
- 1 cup shredded carrots
- 1 cup snow peas
- 2 cups cooked quinoa

Miso Ginger Dressing
- 1- 2 teaspoons honey
- ⅛ teaspoon sea salt
- 2 tablespoons gluten-free tamari
- 1 tablespoon rice vinegar
- 1 tablespoon white miso paste
- 1 teaspoon fresh ginger
- 1 tablespoon lemon juice

Method:
1. Add ½ cup quinoa and ½ cup water in a small saucepan.
2. Get the water to a boil. When boiling, reduce to low heat, cover, and cook for fifteen minutes, or until all of the water has been absorbed.
3. Turn off the heat and allow it to cool for a few minutes after the water has been consumed.
4. In the meantime, prepare the remaining veggies and combine them in a mixing bowl.
5. In a small bowl or fluid quart container, mix all of the ingredients until well mixed.
6. Combine all chopped vegetables, chickpeas, boiled quinoa, and cashew nuts in a big mixing bowl.
7. Toss in the dressing until it is well mixed.

9.5 Tofu Sheet and Toona Sinensis Sprout Salad

Cooking Time: 30 minutes
Serving Size: 2
Ingredients:
- 1 teaspoon dark soy sauce
- 1 tablespoon cornstarch
- 1 scallion
- 1 tablespoon oyster sauce
- 1 pound firm tofu
- ⅛ teaspoon white pepper
- ¼ teaspoon salt
- 3 oz. ground pork
- 1 teaspoon fresh ginger
- 2 teaspoons Shaoxing wine
- 1 oz. salted fish

Method:

1. Ground meat and ginger should be minced together.
2. To create room for the pork, scrape out about 1 teaspoon of tofu from each slice.
3. Toss the leftover tofu with the pork in a mixing dish.
4. Toss the meat mixture with the wine, a sprinkle of freshly roasted white pepper, and salt. Mix thoroughly.
5. Toss the meat with the tofu parts and serve.
6. In a skillet or steamer, steam the tofu sheet for about ten minutes.
7. Set aside one tablespoon of cornflour and one tablespoon of water, whereas the tofu is roasting.
8. Remove the plate cautiously when the tofu is finished.
9. Return any remaining water to the skillet and, if necessary, add more water to make around a quarter cup of liquid.
10. Bring the liquid to a low boil, then add the oyster sauce and light sesame oil.
11. Add salt and pepper, then stir in the cornflour liquid.
12. Garnish with spring onions after pouring the sauce over the tofu.

9.6 Sriracha Chinese Cucumber Salad

Cooking Time: 30 minutes
Serving Size: 4
Ingredients:

- ¼ to ½ teaspoon granulated sugar
- 1 teaspoon sriracha sauce
- 2 cloves garlic minced
- 1 teaspoon sesame oil
- ½ to 1 teaspoon salt
- 4 Persian cucumbers

Optional Garnishes
- ¼ teaspoon red pepper flakes
- ½ teaspoon chopped cilantro

Method:
1. Cucumbers can be cut into parts.
2. Then cut each third laterally in half, and then long ways in half too.
3. Put the cucumbers in a bowl and season with ½ teaspoon salt.
4. Leave them to stay for 30 minutes to allow the salt to pull the water out of the cucumbers.
5. Add in the rest of the ingredients until the cucumbers are completely covered with seasonings.
6. Taste and make any required adjustments.
7. You can eat the cucumbers right away or leave them in the fridge to produce the flavors.

9.7 Cottage Cheese Chinese Salad

Cooking Time: 10 minutes
Serving Size: 4
Ingredients:
- 2 medium cucumbers
- Salt and pepper to taste

- 4 Roma (plum) tomatoes
- 4 green onions
- 1 container cottage cheese

Method:
1. Combine the cottage cheese, peppers, fresh basil, and cucumbers in a medium mixing dish.
2. To taste, sprinkle with salt.
3. Chill until ready to serve.

Chapter 10: Most Famous Chinese Dishes

10.1 Dim Sums

Cooking Time: 1 hour 10 minutes
Serving Size: 4
Ingredients:
For Chicken and Prawn Dumplings
- Potato starch
- Salt
- 2.5 grams white pepper
- Wonton skin
- 150 grams chicken
- 5 grams sugar
- 5 ml sesame oil
- 150 grams prawn

For Vegetable Coriander Dumplings
- 5 grams sugar
- 5 grams sesame oil
- 10ml oil
- 10 grams brown garlic
- 10 grams bamboo shoots
- 10 grams garlic
- 10 grams carrots
- 10 grams water chestnuts
- 10 grams button mushrooms

For Wonton Skin
- 50 grams wheat starch
- Salt
- Potato starch

Method:

1. Combine sugar, pepper, soy sauce, and cornmeal with minced chicken and prawns.
2. Fill the wonton skin with the combination and steam it.
3. However, for the wanton skin, combine all ingredients.
4. Fill the wonton skin with the mixture and steam it.
5. Combine the potato, 50 gm wheat flour, and a bit of salt in a mixing bowl.
6. Stir in hot water until it the slightly thickened.
7. Add potato starch until it binds.
8. Make a roll and cut it into tiny squares by sprinkling wheat starch on top.
9. Then, using a roller, roll the balls into a flat round or shape before adding fillings.
10. 250g red chilies, soaked for three hours to make a paste out of it.
11. Add chili paste, salt, and sugar once the garlic has turned orange.

10.2 Hot and Sour Soup

Cooking Time: 15 minutes
Serving Size: 4

Ingredients:

- ½ teaspoon salt
- 2 tablespoon spring onion
- ½ teaspoon pepper powder
- ½ teaspoon sugar
- 2 tablespoon vinegar
- 1 teaspoon chili sauce
- 4 cup water

- 2 tablespoon soy sauce
- 2 tablespoon oil
- ½ capsicum
- 5 beans
- 2 clove garlic
- 1 carrot
- 3 tablespoon cabbage
- 1-inch ginger
- 2 tablespoon spring onion
- 1 chili

For Corn Flour Slurry
- ¼ cup water
- 2 tablespoon cornflour

Method:
1. First, heat two tablespoons of oil in a large skillet and stir fry two garlic cloves, 1-inch ginger, and one chili.
2. Mix in 2 tablespoons green onion until it loosens.
3. One carrot, cabbage, ½ capsicum, and five beans are also good additions.
4. Combine the water, sesame oil, vinegar, and chili sauce in a mixing bowl.
5. Add spice powder, salt, and oil as well.
6. Boil for three minutes or until the flavors are well absorbed.
7. To make a cornflour slurry, combine two tablespoons of cornflour with ¼ cup water.
8. Mix the slurry into the broth thoroughly.
9. Boil for another two minutes or until the soup has thickened slightly.
10. Finally, stir in 2 tablespoons green onion and serve the hot and sour broth immediately.

10.3 Quick Noodles

Cooking Time: 30 minutes
Serving Size: 2
Ingredients:
- 1 medium carrot
- 3 ounces bean sprouts
- 2 garlic cloves
- 2 green onions
- 1 tablespoon soy sauce
- 2 tablespoons vegetable oil
- 3 ounces egg noodles
- 1 tablespoon Shaoxing wine
- 2 teaspoons dark brown sugar
- 1 teaspoon sriracha
- 2 teaspoons sesame oil
- 2 teaspoons dark soy sauce

Method:
1. Mix sesame oil, dark soy sauce, Shaoxing wine, soy sauce, salt, and sriracha in a small cup. Remove from the heat.
2. A big pot of water should be brought to a boil.
3. Cook the noodles in the broth.
4. Cook for three minutes after adding the noodles.
5. With the remaining one tablespoon oil, bring the skillet to a moderate flame.
6. Sauté the cloves and the white color green parts of the spring onion for about thirty seconds, or until aromatic.
7. Return the noodles, along with the soy sauce mixture, to the pan.
8. Heat for 1 minute more, or until the dark green pieces of the spring onion, carrot ribbons, and black beans are only softened.
9. Switch off the heat and serve.

10.4 Szechwan Chili Chicken

Cooking Time: 45 minutes
Serving Size: 8
Ingredients:
- 1 tablespoon black vinegar
- 2 teaspoon chili oil
- 2 teaspoon white pepper
- Oil (for frying)
- 2-3 spring onions
- 10-12 pieces chicken
- to taste salt
- 5-6 dry red chilies
- 3 tablespoon brown peppercorn
- 3 tablespoon green peppercorn
- 2-3 tablespoon ginger

Method:
1. Cook the chicken in a pan with the ginger until it turns golden.
2. Drain the oil and set it aside for now.
3. Add the onion, fresh basil, green coriander seeds, and dark peppercorns at this stage.
4. Mix in the dry chilies, sesame oil powder, ajino moto, pepper, and chili sauce for five minutes.
5. After another 5-10 minutes of stirring, apply the black vinegar.
6. Stir fry for ten minutes, then serve with green peppercorns as a side dish.
7. Chilli meat Szechwan is ready to eat.

10.5 Spring Rolls

Cooking Time: 50 minutes
Serving Size: 8
Ingredients:
- 3 tablespoons hoisin sauce
- 1 teaspoon peanuts
- 2 ounces rice vermicelli
- 2 tablespoons white sugar
- ½ teaspoon garlic chili sauce
- 8 rice wrappers
- 2 tablespoons fresh lime juice
- 1 clove garlic
- 8 large cooked shrimp
- 4 teaspoons fish sauce
- ¼ cup water
- 1 ⅓ tablespoons Thai basil
- 3 tablespoons cilantro
- 2 leaves lettuce
- 3 tablespoons mint leaves

Method:
1. A small saucepan of water should be brought to a boil.
2. Three to five minutes, or until al dente, simmer rice vermicelli, and rinse.
3. Fill a large mixing bowl halfway with hot water.
4. To loosen one wrapper, place it in the warm water for 1 second.
5. Add two shrimp halves, a pinch of vermicelli, lettuce, basil, coriander, and cabbage in a row across the middle, keeping about 2 inches exposed on each side.

6. Combine the oyster sauce, water, lemon juice, cloves, sugar, and chili sauce in a small cup.
7. Combine the hoisin paste and peanuts in a separate small dish.
8. Serve the rolled spring rolls with a combination of fish sauce and hoisin sauces.

10.6 Stir-Fried Tofu with Rice

Cooking Time: 40 minutes
Serving Size: 4
Ingredients:
For the Tofu
- A handful of coriander leaves
- 1 teaspoon refined oil
- 1-inch red onion, chopped
- 2 teaspoon honey
- 100 grams tofu
- 2 teaspoon soya sauce
- 3 garlic cloves, chopped
- 2 teaspoon chili paste
- 2 shallots
- 1-inch ginger
- 1 lemongrass stick

For the Fried Rice
- Handful of coriander
- 1 teaspoon olive oil
- 2 teaspoon soya sauce
- ½ lemon (squeezed)
- Carrots, chopped
- 1 fresh red chili, chopped
- 1 ginger
- Salt and pepper

- Spring onions

Method:
1. In a hot oven pan, rain distilled oil and add minced mariner, stirring well.
2. Then season with salt and pepper and insert the garlic, cloves, and shallots.
3. Combine the red chili paste, sesame oil, and honey in a cup.
4. Put it all together with some coriander.
5. In a hot oven skillet, drizzle vegetable oil and insert carrots, green onions, ginger, salt, and black pepper.
6. Then combine the fresh red chili, lime juice, and soy sauce in a large mixing bowl.
7. Add some cilantro leaves, sliced.
8. Cook for about 5-7 minutes.
9. It is better served on a platter.

10.7 Shitake Fried Rice with Water Chestnuts

Cooking Time: 25 minutes
Serving Size: 2
Ingredients:
- Small bunch parsley
- 1 big drop of sesame oil
- A dash of rice wine vinegar
- 1 stalk spring onions
- 1 cup shitake mushroom
- A pinch of white pepper
- Salt to season
- 1 big drop of sesame oil

- 1 cup rice (cooked)
- 1 big tablespoon celery
- 1 tablespoon ginger
- 2-3 tablespoon vegetable oil
- ½ medium onion
- 1 big tablespoon of leeks
- Green chilies
- 2-3 water chestnuts
- 4 cloves garlic

Method:

1. Cut the water chestnuts, diced peppers, and shitake mushrooms.
2. Vegetable oil is heated in a wok.
3. Combine the onions, kale, and leeks in a large mixing bowl.
4. Grate the ginger, add the mushrooms, and cut the water chestnuts.
5. Combine the rice, green onions, sesame oil, rice vinegar, cloves, and soy sauce in a mixing bowl.
6. Serve in a bowl after a good stir fry.

10.8 Chicken with Chestnuts

Cooking Time: 50 minutes
Serving Size: 8

Ingredients:

- 3 tablespoons hoisin sauce
- 1 teaspoon peanuts
- 2 tablespoons white sugar
- ½ teaspoon garlic chili sauce
- 2 ounces rice vermicelli
- 2 tablespoons fresh lime juice

- 1 clove garlic, minced
- 8 rice wrappers
- 3 tablespoons cilantro
- 2 leaves lettuce
- 4 teaspoons fish sauce
- 1 ⅓ tablespoons Thai basil
- 3 tablespoons mint leaves
- 8 large cooked shrimp
- ¼ cup water

Method:
1. If needed, cut chicken parts into tiny chunks.
2. Enable chicken to marinate in 2 tablespoons of sesame oil for 10-15 minutes.
3. In a large skillet, heat the oil, add the green onion and ginger, continue cooking until moist.
4. Arrange the chicken parts in a thin layer in the pan.
5. Brown one hand, then flip all of the bits over and brown the other.
6. Add two tablespoons of tomato sauce, sherry, sugar, star anise, soaked in water, shitake mushrooms, and soaking liquid for shitake mushrooms.
7. Combine the sauce and the chicken in a large mixing bowl.
8. Bring to the boil, then decrease to low heat and cook, protected, for 20 minutes.
9. Toss in the chestnuts softly.
10. Cover and continue to cook for an additional 15-20 minutes or until the chicken is soft.

Conclusion

It is no misconception to suggest that "food is a paradise for the citizens" in Chinese. People in China eat tasty food in all sections of life. Cooking has evolved into a complex art form. China is split into 34 provinces, with its rich traditions that reflect its unique landscape, environment, background, and culture. New, local products and seasoning are used to inspire culinary styles. Both of these factors contributed to the creation of the "Eight Delicacies" and "Four Tastes." Crucially, Chinese cuisine is often enjoyed with all of the senses. The presentation and smell of a dish are judged first, followed by the flavor and quality. Moreover, a high-quality dish should have at least one of the following attributes, if not all of them. Chinese Cookbook has a variety of "Chinese Recipes" to choose from. You will have a great chance to experience various local cuisines and improve the taste of your meals at your table.

THAI

COOKBOOK

70 Easy Recipes for Traditional Food from Thailand

Maki Black

The trademarks that are used are without any consent, and the publication of the trademark is without permission or backing by the trademark owner. All trademarks and brands within this book are for clarifying purposes only and are owned by the owners themselves, not affiliated with this document.

Contents

CHAPTER 3: THE WORLD OF TRADITIONAL THAI LUNCH RECIPES................................142

CHAPTER 4: THE WORLD OF TRADITIONAL THAI DINNER RECIPES................................167

Introduction

Food is an indispensable part of our every day schedule. Without the addition of solid, nutritious, and scrumptious food, life can truly transform into a test. Cooking is viewed as a difficult task because of the lack of our cooking abilities or exposure to the authentic recipes of different cuisines.

This book is principally about Thai cuisine. Thai food is the public cooking of Thailand. Thai cooking places accentuation on light meals with amazing aromatic segments and a spicy or zesty edge. Thai cooking is about the shuffling of different components to make an amicable completion i.e. like an unpredictable melodic harmony, it must have a smooth surface, yet it does not make a difference what goes on underneath.

In this cookbook, you will come across the history and origin of Thai food as well as the history of traditional Thai dishes. You are going to get a brief information regarding the evolution of Thai cuisine over the years.

There are various health benefits of having Thai food at home, and you will know all of these benefits when you go through the different properties of spices used in Thai foods. You will get over 70 different breakfast, lunch, dinner, and dessert, and authentic recipes that are only eaten by Thai people. You can easily start cooking at home with the detailed instructions present below each recipe.

Preparing your Thai food at home without the need to order food from some restaurant can become very easy, once you start reading this book. So, why wait for more? Let us dive deep into the world of Thai cuisine.

Chapter 1: Introduction to Thai Food

Thailand is the most hailed country in the whole world for its cuisine. From the southern landmass toward the northern locales, the country offers a diverse blend of an irresistibly delightful food.

The south of Thailand is acclaimed for its blazing curries, profound usage of coconut milk, and astonishing fish plans. The northeastern part is striking for its veggie filled plates of blended greens and flavors, grilled meat, sausages, and tenacious rice. Bangkok, the greatest city, attracts Thais from all over the country to make an endless mix of alluring flavors to taste.

From streak cooked sautés to hand beaten servings of blended greens, you can find the variety of mouthwatering flavors. If you value eating, you will be in a paradise with the combination and variety of food in this cuisine.

1.1 History and Origin of Thai Food

Thai food started with the people who emigrated from the southern Chinese regions many years back to the land of Thailand. There was a great Szechwan impact on Thai cooking. In any case, all through the long haul, various things have affected Thai food.

Previously, Buddhist clerics carried an Indian touch to the food, and southern Muslim states influenced the cooking in the south of Thailand. Much later, Thai food was affected by European cooking after contact with Portuguese clergymen and Dutch merchants. During this Time, there was some effect from the Japanese as well.

Thailand is a significant country with a distinct geography, and all through the long haul, this has provoked the improvement of nearby divergences in its style of food varieties.

1.2 History of Traditional Thai Dishes

In the beginning, Thai food was usually eaten while sitting on mats or covers on the floor. These traditions are still found in the more customary and traditional families. Right now, there are four distinct styles of cooking in Traditional Thai food:

- The focal region of Thailand offers food that is somewhere between the north and south. In any case, fragrant Jasmine rice is liked by numerous individuals in the area.

- Southern Thai cooking is the most standard and traditional style for cooking in Thailand since that is the essential tourist territory of the country. In southern cooking, there is significantly more use of coconut milk in various dishes. Coconut replaces Ghee for fricasseeing, and there is a significant usage of fish in majority of their dishes.

- The cooking in northern Thailand is ordinarily milder than in the rest of the country. Firm rice is liked, usually it is kneaded into little balls with the fingers and this is one of the most traditional dishes of Thailand.

- The food in the north east is affected by Laos. The food is astoundingly spiced, and tenacious glutinous rice is the supported staple for north-eastern dishes. Regardless of the point that there are great deals of meat dishes in this section of Thailand, meat was inadequate in these towns, and the highest of protein were shrimp and freshwater fish.

1.3 Evolution of Thai Food over Time

Customarily, while Thai cooking, you do not have to think much as there are a variety of foods available. Thus, arranging food requires heaps of interest and participation, including the family members to cook it all together. The food explains the Thai life and its traditions, customs, and culture. Thai families are gigantic and well-weave. In cooking, Thai family members help each other as a group. In cooking curries, young people assist with light work like nipping off basil leaves, and adults help in pounding chilies and other flavors.

In the current day, making Thai food is much less difficult as each of the ingredients are expeditiously open in general stores, yet there is an examination that it does not have the standard principles of the past.

1.4 Thai Foods According to Nutrition and Dietetics

Thai food is normally adored in the United States, and this food has some amazing nutritional benefits as well. The traditional eating routine of Thailand features striking vegetables, fish, and meats that are given rice or noodles and arranged with flavors like turmeric, galangal, Thai basil, and lemongrass. Food served at Western Thai eateries shares numerous parts of valid Thai cooking, despite the fact that it has some striking contrasts.

Thai menus in America may have greater fragments, more singed nourishments, and plans that are higher in salt and sugar. Following are the curative advantages of Thai food:

- The most generally utilized veggies in Thai dinners are flavorful, like peppers, tomato, cabbage, broccoli, carrots, and onions. These veggies are stacked with fiber, nutrients, minerals, and an assortment of mixtures that add to great absorption and general wellbeing.

- Several of the most well-known Thai ingredients are nutritious, yet there are other sound parts of Thai food. For one, Thai suppers frequently highlight a decent equilibrium of macronutrients like protein, fats, and carbs.

- Eating dinners which to a great extent involve non-bland veggies and furthermore contain protein and fat can assist you with keeping up stable glucose levels for the whole day. This, thusly, prompts supported energy and may help weight reduction.

- Curries, pan-sears, and soups are made with an assortment of vegetables, incorporate a protein source like tofu, lean meat, or fish, and contain coconut milk, nut sauces, or other good fats.

Thai food is known for joining provincial spices and flavors, vegetables, and lean proteins that add both flavor and nourishments to suppers. Nonetheless, some Westernized Thai dishes are pan fried, served in segments, or contain unreasonable measures of added sugar and salt. To pick a solid Thai feast, decide on a dish that are stacked with plant food varieties, contains a protein source, and highlights an assortment of spices and flavors.

1.5 Key Ingredients Used in Thai Food

A large portion of the ingredients found in Thai food are a clear reflection of the environment warm, fertile land and abundant water.

Recipes contain fish, unusual products of the soil, a few sorts of noodles and sauces. Rice is the mainstay of most meals.

Hot flavoring mixes are utilized to season everything from the day's catch to the easy to make servings of rice or noodles. Following are a portion of the primary ingredients utilized in Thai cooking:

- Cumin: Thai cooks broil fragrant, natural cumin seeds in a dry container to draw out its flavor, and afterward granulate it for use in curry pastes and other zest mixes. Cumin is likewise an essential fixing in many flavor mixes, soups, stews, meat, bean and rice dishes.

- Basil: Basil is utilized both as an enhancing flavor and a topping in Thai cooking. Small bunch of basils are commonly used in soups, curries and sautés.

- Cinnamon: Thai cooks favor Chinese cinnamon, or Cinnamomum cassia, which is better, to some degree spicier, and more uncommon in shading and flavor than Cinnamomum zeylanicum.

- Garlic: Thai cooks use garlic for its health properties, fragrance, and the way that its flavor mixes well with an assortment of different flavors. Garlic is a principle ingredient in the customary Big Four Seasonings Blend, alongside salt, cilantro root, and white peppercorns.

- Cardamom: The fragrant cardamom seedpod is utilized in a couple of Thai dishes of Indian inception, as Mussaman curry. Somewhat lemony, cardamom additionally has a marginally peppery and sweet taste as well as fragrance. Thai cooks frequently consolidate cardamom with other sweet-smelling flavors, similar to cinnamon, nutmeg, and mace.

- Lemongrass: The light, lemony flavor and aroma of lemongrass is an important staple in Thai food. Thai cooks utilize the bulb and base leaves of lemongrass to prepare sauces, soups, pan-sears and curries. It improves meats, poultry, fish, and vegetables, and it is particularly delectable with garlic, chilies and cilantro.

- Turmeric: The robes of Buddhist priests in Thailand are shaded with antiquated yellow color produced using turmeric. Its flavor is sweet, warm, and somewhat peppery. However, it is utilized principally for shading in numerous Thai dishes, including curries, toppings, fish and grain dishes.

- Curry Powders and Pastes: Thais generally mix their own curry powders and pastes by pounding different spices and flavors in a mortar and pestle. Curries are utilized to season coconut milk, serving of mixed greens dressings, noodle sauces, fish and meat dishes, vegetable dishes and soups.

- Chili peppers: Thai food is hot, because of its liberal utilization of new and dried stew peppers. Despite the fact that stew peppers are not local, they are presently fundamental for Thai food.

- Coriander: The strongly fragrant and somewhat interesting kind of coriander seeds is valued in Thai cooking. Thai cooks utilize the root and the leaf of the plant.

- Galangal: A relative of ginger, this light yellow zest has a sharp, lemony, peppery hot taste. It is otherwise called galingale, Java root, or Siamese ginger. Enormous, slim bits of galangal are utilized to season Thai soups, stews and curries; for pastes, it is finely sliced and beat. Ginger might be a replacement for galangal in most Thai plans.

- Mace: It has somewhat nutty, warm taste and found in soups, stuffing, sauces and heated products. It supplements fish, meats, and cheddar, just as certain refreshments.

- Cilantro: Also known as Chinese parsley, Thais utilize this delicate, verdant plant for its unmistakable flavor and natural or amazing fragrance.

- Nutmeg: Thai cooks appreciate the extreme fragrance and sweet, zesty kind of nutmeg in recipes for sweet and appetizing dishes. The chefs utilize a grater to finely powder the nutmeg.

- Cloves: This dim earthy colored, sweet-smelling zest is utilized in the Thai kitchen. Its taste is particular, sharp, and warm or sweet, and you will discover it in both sweet and savory plans.

Thai food will engage any cook who adores the art of seasoning. And while many dishes are very hot, those prepared at home can be adjusted to just the right degree for your own tastes.

Chapter 2: The World of Traditional Thai Breakfast Recipes

Following are some classic traditional Thai breakfast recipes that are rich in healthy nutrients and you can easily make them with the detailed instructions list in each recipe:

2.1 Salapao Recipe

Preparation Time: 30 minutes

Cooking Time: 15 minutes

Serving: 4

Ingredients:

- Sugar, half tablespoon
- Ground pork, half pound
- Soy sauce, one tablespoon
- Finely chopped shallots, one tablespoon
- Chopped garlic, half tablespoon
- Thai pepper powder, half teaspoon

For the dough:

- Vegetable oil, one tablespoon
- Milk, one cup
- Mixed flour, one and a half cup
- Sugar, four tablespoon

Instructions:

1. Take a large bowl.

2. Add the mixed flour and sugar.

3. In a separate bowl, add vegetable oil and the milk.

4. Add the dry ingredients into the wet ingredients.

5. Knead the dough until it turns semi soft.

6. In a pan, add the ground pork.

7. Cook your pork and then add the finely chopped shallots.

8. Cook your pork until the color of the pork changes.

9. Once the color changes, add the soy sauce, sugar, Thai pepper powder and the chopped garlic.

10. Once the pork is done, knead the dough into small round buns.

11. Add the ground pork into the buns and cover the buns all over.

12. Place the buns in the steamer and steam your buns.

13. Steam your buns for ten to fifteen minutes.

14. Your dish is ready to be served.

2.2 Khao Neow Sang Kaya Recipe

Preparation Time: 30 minutes

Cooking Time: 10 minutes

Serving: 4

Ingredients:

- Coconut cream, one cup
- Vanilla extract, one teaspoon
- Eggs, four
- Palm sugar, half cup
- Coconut milk, one cup

Instructions:

1. In a large bowl, add eggs and beat them well.
2. Beat the eggs until it forms a foamy structure.
3. Add the coconut cream and vanilla extract.
4. Beat the mixture and form a fluffy mixture.
5. Add the coconut milk and palm sugar.
6. Mix everything well and form a homogenized mixture.
7. Add the mixture into a greased pan.
8. Add the pan into a steamer.
9. Steam your mixture for ten minutes.
10. Dish out your mixture and cut into pieces.
11. Your dish is ready to be served.

2.3 Khanum Pang (Thai Waffles) Recipe

Preparation Time: 30 minutes

Cooking Time: 10 minutes

Serving: 4

Ingredients:

- Rice flour, one cup
- Eggs, two
- Chopped fresh cilantro, half cup
- Coconut milk, one cup
- Salt to taste
- Shredded coconut, half cup
- Cardamom powder, two tablespoon

Instructions:

1. Heat your waffle maker.
2. Always remember you heat your waffle maker till the point that it starts producing steam.
3. Remove the egg whites in a bowl and beat them to the point that they become fluffy.
4. Beat the egg yolks in a separate bowl.
5. Add in the egg yolks in the egg whites and delicately mix them with a spatula.
6. Combine the eggs and the rest of the ingredients.
7. When your waffle maker is heated adequately, pour in the mixture.

8. Close your waffle maker.

9. Let your waffle cook for five to six minutes approximately.

10.   When your waffles are done, dish them out.

11.   Add on top of the waffles the chopped cilantro leaves.

12.   Your dish is ready to be served.

2.4 Khanom Recipe

Preparation Time: 30 minutes

Cooking Time: 25 minutes

Serving: 4

Ingredients:

- Cornstarch, three tablespoon
- Salt, as required
- Fresh chopped chives, two tablespoon
- Full-fat coconut milk, two cups
- Unsweetened shredded coconut, a quarter cup
- Rice flour, two cups
- Sugar, half cup
- White rice (cooked), three tablespoon
- Canola oil, as required

Instructions:

1. In a large bowl add the coconut milk.

2. With the help of an electrical beater, beat the coconut milk for approximately ten minutes.

3. You will see that after ten minutes, the coconut milk would be fluffy.

4. In a grinder, add the white rice and unsweetened shredded coconut.

5. Grind your ingredients into a fine paste without any granules.

6. Now add this mixture into the beaten coconut milk.

7. Fold your mixture well.

8. Add the rice flour, cornstarch and sugar into the mixture.

9. The mixture will become a little heavier but remember not to beat the mixture, rather fold it so the air spaces are kept intact.

10. Mix all the left ingredients into the coconut milk mixture.

11. In a muffin tray, add your coconut milk mixture.

12. Grease the muffin tray with canola oil.

13. Steam your mixture for approximately ten to fifteen minutes.

14. When your khanom is cooked, dish it out.

15. Your dish is ready to be served.

2.5 Khai Luak (Thai Soft Eggs) Recipe

Preparation Time: 30 minutes

Cooking Time: 10 minutes

Serving: 4

Ingredients:

- Vegetable oil, one and a half tablespoon
- Cooked pork chops, one cup
- Eggs, four
- Sliced scallions, four
- Sliced shallots, two medium sized
- Cooked barley, one cup
- Fresh coriander leaves, half cup
- Fish sauce, one tablespoon
- Lime juice, two tablespoon
- Sliced red chili, one long

Instructions:

1. In a medium bowl, mix together the lime juice, fish sauce, one teaspoon of the chili paste, and the cooked grains.

2. Put the eggs and the excess half teaspoon of chili paste in a little bowl.

3. Beat with a fork to mix everything.

4. In a huge weighty sauté dish, heat half tablespoon of the oil over medium-high warmth.

5. Add the shallots, the white areas of the scallions, and the pork, (if utilizing) and cook, blending infrequently, until the shallots are dim earthy colored and withered.

6. Cook for four more minutes.

7. Add the scallion greens and the leftover half tablespoon of oil and cook briefly.

8. Pour in the egg blend and cook for thirty seconds, at that point turn and mix your eggs.

9. Pour in the mixture of the grain and cook, turning with a spatula, until it is cooked properly.

10. Your dish is ready to be served.

2.6 Khao Rad Gyang (Thai Breakfast Rice and Curry) Recipe

Preparation Time: 30 minutes

Cooking Time: 10 minutes

Serving: 4

Ingredients:

- Thai chilies, two
- Jalapeno, one large
- Sliced green onions, half cup
- White peppercorns, one teaspoon
- Cilantro, one cup

- Fresh ginger, one teaspoon
- Fish sauce, one tablespoon
- Soy sauce, one tablespoon
- Chinese 5 spice, half teaspoon
- Chili garlic sauce, two tablespoon
- Fresh cilantro leaves, half cup
- Thai basil leaves, a quarter cup
- Beef broth, one can
- Minced lemon grass, one teaspoon
- Egg, one large
- Cooked rice, as required

Instructions:

1. Add all the ingredients of the curry into a pan.
2. Add the beef broth and sauces into the mixture.
3. Cook your dish for ten minutes.
4. Add the cooked rice into the mixture once the curry is ready.
5. Mix the rice well and cook it for five minutes.
6. Add the egg into the pan by pushing the rest of the ingredients to a side.
7. Cook the egg and then mix the rest of the ingredients into it.
8. Cook your dish for five more minutes.
9. Add the cilantro into the dish.
10. Mix your rice and then dish it out.

11.   Your dish is ready to be served.

2.7 Khao Yum (Thai Breakfast Rice Salad) Recipe

Preparation Time: 10 minutes

Cooking Time: 30 minutes

Serving: 4

Ingredients:

- Water, two tablespoon
- Turmeric powder, one pinch
- Salt to taste
- Garlic cloves, four
- Cooked rice, one cup
- Mix veggies, one cup
- Olive oil

For Thai Dressing:

- Fish sauce, half tablespoon
- Brown sugar, half tablespoon
- Chopped small chili, one
- Water, one tablespoon
- Peanut oil, one teaspoon
- Rice vinegar, half tablespoon
- Sweet chili sauce, half tablespoon

Instructions:

1. Take a large bowl.
2. Add the ingredients for the dressing into the bowl.
3. Mix everything well enough to form a homogeneous mixture.
4. In the next bowl, add the ingredients for the salad.
5. Add the ingredients for the salad into a pan.
6. Cook your ingredients for five to ten minutes.
7. Add the ingredients into a bowl.
8. Add the dressing on top and mix all the ingredients well.
9. Your dish is ready to be served.

2.8 Thai Breakfast Rice and Shrimp Soup Recipe

Preparation Time: 30 minutes

Cooking Time: 10 minutes

Serving: 4

Ingredients:

- White peppercorns, one teaspoon
- Cilantro, one cup
- Shrimps, 150 grams
- Fish sauce, one tablespoon
- Soy sauce, one and a half tablespoon

- Pork stock, three cup
- Jasmine rice, four cups
- Garlic cloves, four

Instructions:

1. Crush the white peppercorns until they turn into powdered form.
2. At that point, add garlic and cilantro and pound until they are crushed.
3. Add portion of this paste to your shrimps and blend well.
4. Sauté the shrimps in a dish with a drop of oil just until it is cooked through.
5. Deglaze the container with some stock and scratch any pieces of spice adhered to the base.
6. Remove from skillet.
7. Bring the stock to a bubble in a pot, add the other portion of the spice paste and stew briefly.
8. Season with fish sauce and soy sauce, at that point taste and add more if you prefer.
9. When prepared to serve, heat the stock to the point of boiling.
10. Add the rice and the shrimp into the stock.
11. Add the soup into a bowl.
12. Garnish it with cilantro leaves.
13. Your dish is ready to be served.

2.9 Thai Styled Traditional Omelet Recipe

Preparation Time: 30 minutes

Cooking Time: 10 minutes

Serving: 4

Ingredients:

- Bean sprouts, one cup
- Fresh coriander leaves, half cup
- Fish sauce, one tablespoon
- Lime juice, two tablespoon
- Sliced red chili, one long
- Green beans, one cup
- Vegetable oil, one and a half tablespoon
- Sliced mushrooms, one cup
- Eggs, eight
- Sliced red capsicum, one large
- Chopped tomatoes, two medium sized

Instructions:

1. Beat the eggs, quarter cup water, lime juice, fish sauce and a large portion of the chili in an enormous container.

2. Heat two teaspoons of oil in a medium non-stick skillet over medium-high warmth.

3. Cook capsicum and mushrooms, mix, for five minutes or until brilliant and delicate.

4. Add the tomatoes.

5. Cook, mixing, for two minutes or until marginally softened.

6. Boil your green beans in water and then drain them.

7. Combine the mushroom blend, sprouts and beans in a bowl.

8. Warm one teaspoon of residual oil in skillet over medium-high heat.

9. Pour quarter of the egg blend into a dish.

10. Cook for thirty seconds or until just set.

11. Slide the omelet onto a plate.

12. Cover your egg to keep it warm.

13. Garnish by sprinkling with coriander and chili.

14. Your dish is ready to be served.

2.10 Thai Breakfast Ginger and Rice Soup Recipe

Preparation Time: 30 minutes

Cooking Time: 10 minutes

Serving: 4

Ingredients:

- White peppercorns, one teaspoon
- Cilantro, one cup
- Ginger paste, two tablespoon
- Fish sauce, one tablespoon
- Soy sauce, one and a half tablespoon
- Pork stock, three cup
- Jasmine rice, four cups
- Garlic cloves, four

Instructions:

1. Crush the white peppercorns until they turn into powdered form.
2. At that point add garlic and cilantro and pound until they are crushed.
3. Add portion of this paste to your ginger paste and blend well.
4. Bring the stock to a bubble in a pot, add the other portion of the spice paste and stew briefly.
5. Season with fish sauce and soy sauce, at that point taste and add more if you prefer.
6. When prepared to serve, heat the stock to the point of boiling.
7. Add the rice and the ginger paste into the stock.
8. Add the soup into a bowl.
9. Garnish it with cilantro leaves.
10. Your dish is ready to be served.

2.11 Spicy Thai Breakfast Noodles Recipe

Preparation Time: 30 minutes

Cooking Time: 10 minutes

Serving: 4

Ingredients:

- Thai chilies, two
- Jalapeno, one large
- Sliced green onions, half cup
- White peppercorns, one teaspoon
- Cilantro, one cup
- Fresh ginger, one teaspoon
- Fish sauce, one tablespoon
- Soy sauce, one tablespoon
- Chinese 5 spice, half teaspoon
- Chili garlic sauce, two tablespoon
- Fresh cilantro leaves, half cup
- Thai basil leaves, a quarter cup
- Beef broth, one can
- Minced lemon grass, one teaspoon
- Egg, one large
- Cooked noodles, as required

Instructions:

1. Add all the ingredients of the sauce into a pan.
2. Add the beef broth and sauces into the mixture.
3. Cook your dish for ten minutes.
4. Add the cooked noodles into the mixture once the sauce is ready.
5. Mix the noodles well and cook it for five minutes.
6. Add the egg into the pan by pushing the rest of the ingredients to a side.
7. Cook the egg and then mix the rest of the ingredients into it.
8. Cook your dish for five more minutes.
9. Add the cilantro into the dish.
10. Mix your noodles and then dish it out.
11. Your dish is ready to be served.

2.12 Thai Fried Eggs Recipe

Preparation Time: 30 minutes

Cooking Time: 10 minutes

Serving: 4

Ingredients:

- Spring onions, four

- Tortilla, as required
- Pepper to taste
- Butter, as required
- Salt to taste
- Baby plum tomatoes, four
- Eggs, four
- Cilantro, half cup

Instructions:

1. Put the butter in a pan.
2. Add the spring onions and chili into the small pan.
3. Cook for a couple of minutes until softened.
4. Whisk the milk and eggs in a bowl.
5. Add the eggs to the pan.
6. Fry your eggs.
7. Add the tomatoes and coriander leaves on top.
8. Once cooked, dish it out.
9. Your dish is ready to be served.

Chapter 3: The World of Traditional Thai Lunch Recipes

Following are some classic traditional Thai lunch recipes that are rich in healthy nutrients and you can easily make them with the detailed instructions list in each recipe:

3.1 Thai Coconut and Noodle Soup Recipe

Preparation Time: 30 minutes

Cooking Time: 10 minutes

Serving: 4

Ingredients:

- Galangal, one can
- Chicken stock, two cups
- Minced garlic, one teaspoon
- Palm sugar, two tablespoon
- Shallot, one
- Kaffir lime leaves, four
- Lime wedges
- Lemon grass, two sticks
- Fish sauce, two tablespoon
- Mushrooms, one cup
- Coconut milk, one cup
- Cilantro, a quarter cup

- Noodles, half pound
- Olive oil, one tablespoon

Instructions:

1. Take a large sauce pan.
2. Add the shallots and olive oil.
3. Cook your shallots and then add the mushrooms.
4. When the mushrooms are cooked then add the galangal, chicken stock, and minced garlic.
5. Add the palm sugar and coconut milk.
6. Cook your ingredients until it starts boiling.
7. Add in the noodles, lemon grass and rest of the ingredients into your soup.
8. Cook your ingredients for ten minutes.
9. When your noodles are cooked dish out your soup.
10. Garnish it with cilantro leaves.
11. Your dish is ready to be served.

3.2 Thai Curry Mud Crab Recipe

Preparation Time: 30 minutes

Cooking Time: 10 minutes

Serving: 4

Ingredients:

- Galangal, one can
- Chicken stock, two cups
- Minced garlic, one teaspoon
- Minced ginger, one teaspoon
- Palm sugar, two tablespoon
- Shallot, one
- Kaffir lime leaves, four
- Lime wedges
- Lemon grass, two sticks
- Fish sauce, two tablespoon
- Mix vegetables, one cup
- Coconut milk, one cup
- Cilantro, a quarter cup
- Crab meat, half pound
- Olive oil, one tablespoon

Instructions:

1. Take a large sauce pan.
2. Add the shallots and olive oil.
3. Cook your shallots and then add the vegetables.
4. When the vegetables are cooked then add the galangal, chicken stock, minced garlic and ginger.
5. Add the palm sugar and coconut milk.
6. Cook your ingredients until it starts boiling.

7. Add in the crab meat, lemon grass and rest of the ingredients into your curry.

8. Cook your ingredients for ten minutes.

9. When your crab meat is cooked dish out your curry.

10.   Garnish it with cilantro leaves.

11.   Your dish is ready to be served.

3.3 Thai Chicken and Sweet Potato Soup Recipe

Preparation Time: 30 minutes

Cooking Time: 10 minutes

Serving: 4

Ingredients:

- Galangal, one can
- Chicken stock, two cups
- Minced garlic, one teaspoon
- Palm sugar, two tablespoon
- Shallot, one
- Kaffir lime leaves, four
- Lime wedges
- Lemon grass, two sticks
- Fish sauce, two tablespoon
- Sweet potatoes, one cup
- Coconut milk, one cup

- Cilantro, a quarter cup
- Chicken meat, half pound
- Olive oil, one tablespoon

Instructions:

1. Take a large sauce pan.
2. Add the shallots and olive oil.
3. Cook your shallots and then add the chicken meat.
4. When the chicken meat is half cooked, add the galangal, chicken stock, and minced garlic.
5. Add the palm sugar and coconut milk.
6. Cook your ingredients until it starts boiling.
7. Add in the sweet potato, lemon grass and rest of the ingredients into your soup.
8. Cook your ingredients for ten minutes.
9. When your sweet potatoes are cooked dish out your soup.
10. Garnish it with cilantro leaves.
11. Your dish is ready to be served.

3.4 Thai Pork and Peanut Curry Recipe

Preparation Time: 30 minutes

Cooking Time: 10 minutes

Serving: 4

Ingredients:

- Galangal, one can
- Chicken stock, two cups
- Minced garlic, one teaspoon
- Minced ginger, one teaspoon
- Chopped onion, half cup
- Kaffir lime leaves, four
- Minced ginger, half tablespoon
- Lemon grass, two sticks
- Fish sauce, two tablespoon
- Peanuts, one cup
- Coconut milk, one cup
- Cilantro, a quarter cup
- Pork meat, half pound
- Olive oil, one tablespoon

Instructions:

1. Take a large sauce pan.

2. Add the chopped onion and olive oil.

3. Cook your chopped onion and then add the pork meat.

4. When the pork meat is half cooked then add the galangal, chicken stock, minced garlic and ginger.

5. Add the coconut milk.

6. Cook your ingredients until it starts boiling.

7. Add in the peanuts, lemon grass and rest of the ingredients into your curry.

8. Cook your ingredients for ten minutes.

9. When the pork meat is cooked completely, dish out your curry.

10. Garnish it with cilantro leaves.

11. Your dish is ready to be served.

3.5 Thai Beef Stir-Fry Recipe

Preparation Time: 10 minutes

Cooking Time: 20 minutes

Serving: 4

Ingredients:

- Fish sauce, two tablespoon
- Soy sauce, half cup

- Beef pieces, three cups
- Tomatoes, two
- Cilantro, half cup
- Salt and pepper, to taste
- Minced ginger, half tablespoon
- Vegetable oil, two tablespoon
- Thai chili peppers, three
- Toasted nuts, half cup
- Onion, one
- Scallions, half cup
- Minced garlic, one teaspoon

Instructions:

1. In a large sauce pan add the shallots and oil.
2. Cook your shallots and then add the ginger and garlic.
3. Cook your ginger and garlic and then add in the beef pieces.
4. Stir fry your beef pieces well.
5. Add all the spices and the rest of the ingredients into your dish except the toasted nuts.
6. When your beef is cooked then add the toasted nuts.
7. Cook your dish for five minutes.
8. Garnish your dish with cilantro.
9. Your dish is ready to be served.

3.6 Thai Minced Chicken Salad Recipe

Preparation Time: 10 minutes

Cooking Time: 20 minutes

Serving: 4

Ingredients:

- Water, two tablespoon
- Turmeric powder, one pinch
- Salt to taste
- Garlic cloves, four
- Cooked chicken mince, one cup
- Olive oil

For Thai Dressing:
- Fish sauce, half tablespoon
- Brown sugar, half tablespoon
- Chopped small chili, one
- Water, one tablespoon
- Peanut oil, one teaspoon
- Rice vinegar, half tablespoon
- Sweet chili sauce, half tablespoon

Instructions:

1. Take a large bowl.
2. Add the ingredients for the dressing into the bowl.
3. Mix everything well enough to form a consistent mixture.
4. In the next bowl, add the ingredients for the salad.
5. Add the ingredients for the salad into a pan.
6. Cook your ingredients for five to ten minutes.
7. Add the ingredients into a bowl.
8. Add the dressing on top and mix all the ingredients well.
9. Your dish is ready to be served.

3.7 Thai Lemongrass Beef Stew with Noodles Recipe

Preparation Time: 30 minutes

Cooking Time: 10 minutes

Serving: 4

Ingredients:

- Galangal, one can
- Beef stock, two cups
- Minced garlic, one teaspoon
- Palm sugar, two tablespoon
- Shallot, one

- Ginger pieces, a quarter cup
- Beef pieces, half pound
- Kaffir lime leaves, four
- Lemon grass, two sticks
- Fish sauce, two tablespoon
- Mixed vegetables, one cup
- Coconut milk, one cup
- Cilantro, a quarter cup
- Noodles, half pound
- Olive oil, one tablespoon

Instructions:

1. Take a large sauce pan.
2. Add the shallots and olive oil.
3. Cook your shallots and then add the mixed vegetables.
4. When the vegetables are cooked then add the galangal, beef stock, and minced garlic.
5. Add the ginger pieces and coconut milk.
6. Cook your ingredients until it starts boiling.
7. Add in the noodles, lemon grass and rest of the ingredients into your soup.
8. Cook your ingredients for ten minutes.
9. When your noodles are cooked dish out your soup.
10. Garnish it with cilantro leaves.
11. Your dish is ready to be served.

3.8 Thai Butternut Squash Soup Recipe

Preparation Time: 30 minutes

Cooking Time: 10 minutes

Serving: 4

Ingredients:

- Galangal, one can
- vegetables stock, two cups
- Minced garlic, one teaspoon
- Palm sugar, two tablespoon
- Shallot, one
- Ginger pieces, a quarter cup
- Butternut squash, half pound
- Kaffir lime leaves, four
- Lemon grass, two sticks
- Fish sauce, two tablespoon
- Coconut milk, one cup
- Cilantro, a quarter cup
- Noodles, half pound
- Olive oil, one tablespoon

Instructions:

1. Take a large sauce pan.
2. Add the shallots and olive oil.
3. Cook your shallots and then add the butternut squash.
4. When the squash is cooked then add the galangal, vegetable stock, and minced garlic.
5. Add the ginger pieces and coconut milk.
6. Cook your ingredients until it starts boiling.
7. Add in the lemon grass and rest of the ingredients into your soup.
8. Cook your ingredients for ten minutes.
9. Garnish it with cilantro leaves.
10. Your dish is ready to be served.

3.9 Thai Green Chicken Soup Recipe

Preparation Time: 30 minutes

Cooking Time: 10 minutes

Serving: 4

Ingredients:

- Galangal, one can
- Chicken stock, two cups
- Minced garlic, one teaspoon
- Palm sugar, two tablespoon

- Shallot, one
- Kaffir lime leaves, four
- Lime wedges
- Lemon grass, two sticks
- Fish sauce, two tablespoon
- Thai green curry paste, two tablespoon
- Coconut milk, one cup
- Cilantro, a quarter cup
- Chicken meat, half pound
- Olive oil, one tablespoon

Instructions:

1. Take a large sauce pan.
2. Add the shallots and olive oil.
3. Cook your shallots and then add the chicken meat.
4. When the chicken meat is half cooked, add the galangal, green curry paste, chicken stock, and minced garlic.
5. Add the palm sugar and coconut milk.
6. Cook your ingredients until it starts boiling.
7. Add in the lemon grass and rest of the ingredients into your soup.
8. Cook your ingredients for ten minutes.
9. When your chicken meat is cooked completely, dish out your soup.
10. Garnish it with cilantro leaves.

11.   Your dish is ready to be served.

3.10 Thai Baked Chicken and Rice Recipe

Preparation Time: 30 minutes

Cooking Time: 25 minutes

Serving: 4

Ingredients:

- Minced ginger, two tablespoon
- Cilantro, half cup
- Olive oil, two tablespoon
- Chopped tomatoes, one cup
- Powdered cumin, one tablespoon
- Salt, to taste
- Black pepper, to taste
- Turmeric powder, one teaspoon
- Fresh Thai herbs, two tablespoon
- Onion, one cup
- Smoked paprika, half teaspoon
- Whole chicken, one pound
- Minced garlic, two tablespoon
- Cooked jasmine rice, as required

Instructions:

1. Take a pan.
2. Add in the oil and onions.
3. Cook the onions until they become soft and fragrant.
4. Add in the chopped garlic and ginger.
5. Cook the mixture and add the tomatoes into it.
6. Add the spices.
7. When the tomatoes are done, add the chicken into it.
8. Mix the chicken so that the tomatoes and spices are coated all over the chicken.
9. Place the chicken on a baking tray and cover your chicken with aluminum foil.
10. Place fresh Thai herbs in the chicken.
11. Bake your chicken for fifteen to twenty minutes.
12. When your chicken is done, dish it out.
13. Sprinkle the cilantro on top of the chicken.
14. Cut your chicken into pieces and place it on the jasmine rice.
15. Your dish is ready to be served.

3.11 Thai Pork Belly with Basil and Tofu Recipe

Preparation Time: 30 minutes

Cooking Time: 10 minutes

Serving: 4

Ingredients:

- Thai chilies, two
- Jalapeno, one large
- Sliced green onions, half cup
- Pork belly pieces, two cups
- Tofu cubes, two cups
- White peppercorns, one teaspoon
- Cilantro, one cup
- Fresh ginger, one teaspoon
- Fish sauce, one tablespoon
- Soy sauce, one tablespoon
- Chinese 5 spice, half teaspoon
- Chili garlic sauce, two tablespoon
- Fresh cilantro leaves, half cup
- Thai basil leaves, a quarter cup
- Chicken broth, one can
- Minced lemon grass, one teaspoon

Instructions:

1. Add all the ingredients of the sauce into a pan.
2. Add the chicken broth and sauces into the mixture.
3. Cook your dish for ten minutes.
4. Add the pork belly pieces and tofu pieces into the mixture once the sauce is ready.

5. Mix the ingredients well and cook it for five minutes.

6. Add the basil leaves and then mix the rest of the ingredients into it.

7. Cook your dish for five more minutes.

8. Add the cilantro into the dish.

9. Your dish is ready to be served.

3.12 Thai Red Meatball Curry Recipe

Preparation Time: 30 minutes

Cooking Time: 10 minutes

Serving: 4

Ingredients:

- Galangal, one can
- Chicken stock, two cups
- Minced garlic, one teaspoon
- Palm sugar, two tablespoon
- Shallot, one
- Kaffir lime leaves, four
- Lime wedges
- Lemon grass, two sticks
- Fish sauce, two tablespoon
- Thai red curry paste, two tablespoon
- Coconut milk, one cup

- Cilantro, a quarter cup
- Frozen meatballs, half pound
- Olive oil, one tablespoon

Instructions:

1. Take a large sauce pan.
2. Add the shallots and olive oil.
3. Cook your shallots and then add the meatballs.
4. When the meatballs are half cooked, add the galangal, red curry paste, chicken stock, and minced garlic.
5. Add the palm sugar and coconut milk.
6. Cook your ingredients until it starts boiling.
7. Add in the lemon grass and rest of the ingredients into the curry.
8. Cook your ingredients for ten minutes.
9. When your curry is cooked dish it out.
10. Garnish it with cilantro leaves.
11. Your dish is ready to be served.

3.13 Thai Sesame Chicken Salad Recipe

Preparation Time: 10 minutes

Cooking Time: 20 minutes

Serving: 4

Ingredients:

- White sesame seeds, half cup
- Black sesame seeds, half cup
- Salt to taste
- Garlic cloves, four
- Cooked chicken meat, one cup
- Olive oil

For Thai Dressing:

- Fish sauce, half tablespoon
- Brown sugar, half tablespoon
- Chopped small chili, one
- Water, one tablespoon
- Peanut oil, one teaspoon
- Rice vinegar, half tablespoon
- Sweet chili sauce, half tablespoon

Instructions:

1. Take a large bowl.
2. Add the ingredients for the dressing into the bowl.
3. Mix everything well enough to form a smooth mixture.
4. In the next bowl, add the ingredients for the salad.
5. Add the ingredients for the salad into a bowl.

6. Add the dressing on top and mix all the ingredients well.

7. Your dish is ready to be served.

3.14 Spicy Thai Prawn Noodles Recipe

Preparation Time: 30 minutes

Cooking Time: 10 minutes

Serving: 4

Ingredients:

- Thai chilies, two
- Jalapeno, one large
- Sliced green onions, half cup
- White peppercorns, one teaspoon
- Cilantro, one cup
- Fresh ginger, one teaspoon
- Fish sauce, one tablespoon
- Soy sauce, one tablespoon
- Chinese 5 spice, half teaspoon
- Chili garlic sauce, two tablespoon
- Fresh cilantro leaves, half cup
- Prawns, two cups
- Fish broth, one can
- Minced lemon grass, one teaspoon
- Cooked noodles, as required

Instructions:

1. Add all the ingredients of the sauce into a pan.
2. Add the fish broth and sauces into the mixture.
3. Cook your dish for ten minutes.
4. Add the cooked noodles into the mixture once the sauce is ready.
5. Mix the noodles well and cook it for five minutes.
6. Add the prawns into the pan by pushing the rest of the ingredients to a side.
7. Cook the prawns and then mix the rest of the ingredients into it.
8. Cook your dish for five more minutes.
9. Add the cilantro into the dish.
10. Mix your noodles and then dish it out.
11. Your dish is ready to be served.

3.15 Thai Red Salmon Curry Recipe

Preparation Time: 30 minutes

Cooking Time: 10 minutes

Serving: 4

Ingredients:

- Galangal, one can
- Fish stock, two cups
- Minced garlic, one teaspoon
- Shallot, one

- Kaffir lime leaves, four
- Lemon grass, two sticks
- Fish sauce, two tablespoon
- Thai red curry paste, two tablespoon
- Cilantro, a quarter cup
- Salmon meat, half pound
- Olive oil, one tablespoon

Instructions:

1. Take a large sauce pan.
2. Add the shallots and olive oil.
3. Cook your shallots and then add the salmon meat.
4. When the salmon meat is half cooked, add the galangal, red curry paste, fish stock, and minced garlic.
5. Cook your ingredients until it starts boiling.
6. Add in the lemon grass and rest of the ingredients into the curry.
7. Cook your ingredients for ten minutes.
8. When your curry is cooked dish it out.
9. Garnish it with cilantro leaves.
10. Your dish is ready to be served.

Chapter 4: The World of Traditional Thai Dinner Recipes

Following are some classic traditional Thai dinner recipes that are rich in healthy nutrients and you can easily make them with the detailed instructions list in each recipe:

4.1 Thai Peanut Chicken and Noodles Recipe

Preparation Time: 30 minutes

Cooking Time: 10 minutes

Serving: 4

Ingredients:

- Galangal, one can
- Chicken stock, two cups
- Minced garlic, one teaspoon
- Minced ginger, one teaspoon
- Chopped onion, half cup
- Noodles, two cups
- Minced ginger, half tablespoon
- Lemon grass, two sticks
- Fish sauce, two tablespoon
- Peanuts, one cup
- Coconut milk, one cup

- Cilantro, a quarter cup
- Chicken meat, half pound
- Olive oil, one tablespoon

Instructions:

1. Take a large sauce pan.
2. Add the chopped onion and olive oil.
3. Cook your chopped onion and then add the chicken meat.
4. When the chicken meat is half cooked then add the galangal, chicken stock, minced garlic and ginger.
5. Add the coconut milk.
6. Cook your ingredients until it starts boiling.
7. Add in the noodles, peanuts, lemon grass and rest of the ingredients into your curry.
8. Cook your ingredients for ten minutes.
9. Garnish it with cilantro leaves.
10. Your dish is ready to be served.

4.2 Thai Red Curry Chicken and Vegetable Recipe

Preparation Time: 30 minutes

Cooking Time: 10 minutes

Serving: 4

Ingredients:

- Galangal, one can
- Chicken stock, two cups
- Minced garlic, one teaspoon
- Shallot, one
- Mix vegetables, one cup
- Lemon grass, two sticks
- Fish sauce, two tablespoon
- Thai red curry paste, two tablespoon
- Cilantro, a quarter cup
- Chicken meat, half pound
- Olive oil, one tablespoon

Instructions:

1. Take a large sauce pan.
2. Add the shallots and olive oil.
3. Cook your shallots and then add the chicken meat and vegetables.
4. When the chicken meat is half cooked, add the galangal, red curry paste, chicken stock, and minced garlic.
5. Cook your ingredients until it starts boiling.
6. Add in the lemon grass and rest of the ingredients into the dish.
7. Cook your ingredients for ten minutes.

8. Garnish it with cilantro leaves.

9. Your dish is ready to be served.

4.3 Thai Noodles with Spicy Peanut Sauce Recipe

Preparation Time: 30 minutes

Cooking Time: 10 minutes

Serving: 4

Ingredients:

- Mixed vegetables, two cups
- Minced garlic, one teaspoon
- Minced ginger, one teaspoon
- Chopped onion, half cup
- Noodles, two cups
- Minced ginger, half tablespoon
- Lemon grass, two sticks
- Fish sauce, two tablespoon
- Spicy peanut sauce, one cup
- Coconut milk, one cup
- Cilantro, a quarter cup
- Olive oil, one tablespoon

Instructions:

1. Take a large sauce pan.
2. Add the chopped onion and olive oil.
3. Cook your chopped onion and then add the vegetables.
4. Add the coconut milk.
5. Cook your ingredients until it starts boiling.
6. Add in the noodles, spicy peanut sauce and the rest of the ingredients.
7. Cook your ingredients for ten minutes.
8. Garnish it with cilantro leaves.
9. Your dish is ready to be served.

4.4 Thai Coconut and Beef Curry Recipe

Preparation Time: 30 minutes

Cooking Time: 10 minutes

Serving: 4

Ingredients:

- Galangal, one can
- Beef stock, two cups
- Minced garlic, one teaspoon
- Crushed ginger, one teaspoon
- Chopped onion, half cup
- Minced ginger, half tablespoon
- Lemon grass, two sticks

- Fish sauce, two tablespoon
- Shredded coconut, one cup
- Coconut milk, one cup
- Cilantro, a quarter cup
- Beef meat, half pound
- Olive oil, one tablespoon

Instructions:

1. Take a large sauce pan.
2. Add the chopped onion and olive oil.
3. Cook your chopped onion and then add the beef meat.
4. When the beef meat is half cooked then add the galangal, beef stock, minced garlic and ginger.
5. Add the coconut milk.
6. Cook your ingredients until it starts boiling.
7. Add in the shredded coconut, lemon grass and rest of the ingredients into your curry.
8. Cook your ingredients for ten minutes.
9. When your beef meat is cooked completely dish out your curry.
10. Garnish it with cilantro leaves.
11. Your dish is ready to be served.

4.5 Thai Coconut and Beef Salad Recipe

Preparation Time: 10 minutes

Cooking Time: 20 minutes

Serving: 4

Ingredients:

- Water, two tablespoon
- Shredded coconut, half cup
- Salt to taste
- Garlic cloves, four
- Cooked beef strips, one cup
- Olive oil

For Thai Dressing:

- Fish sauce, half tablespoon
- Brown sugar, half tablespoon
- Chopped small chili, one
- Water, one tablespoon
- Peanut oil, one teaspoon
- Rice vinegar, half tablespoon
- Sweet chili sauce, half tablespoon

Instructions:

1. Take a large bowl.
2. Add the ingredients for the dressing into the bowl.
3. Mix everything well enough to form a consistent mixture.
4. In the next bowl, add the ingredients for the salad.

5. Add the ingredients for the salad into a bowl and mix properly.

6. Add the dressing on top and mix all the ingredients well.

7. Your dish is ready to be served.

4.6 Thai Green Chicken Thighs Recipe

Preparation Time: 10 minutes

Cooking Time: 40 minutes

Serving: 2

Ingredients:

- Chicken broth, one cup
- Thai green curry paste, one teaspoon
- Onion, one cup
- Lemon juice, half cup
- Chicken thighs, half pound
- Thai spices, half tablespoon
- Water, one cup
- Minced garlic, two tablespoon
- Minced ginger, two tablespoon
- Cilantro, half cup
- Olive oil, two tablespoon

- Chopped tomatoes, one cup

Instructions:

1. Take a pan.
2. Add in the oil and onions.
3. Cook the onions until they become soft and fragrant.
4. Add in the chopped garlic and ginger.
5. Cook the mixture and add the tomatoes into it.
6. Add the spices and chicken thighs.
7. Add in the broth.
8. Mix the ingredients carefully and cover your pan.
9. Add cilantro on top.
10. Your dish is ready to be served.

4.7 Thai Basil Pork Stir-Fry Recipe

Preparation Time: 10 minutes

Cooking Time: 20 minutes

Serving: 4

Ingredients:

- Fish sauce, two tablespoon
- Soy sauce, half cup
- Pork pieces, three cups
- Tomatoes, two

- Cilantro, half cup
- Salt and pepper, to taste
- Minced ginger, half tablespoon
- Vegetable oil, two tablespoon
- Thai chili peppers, three
- Basil leaves, half cup
- Onion, one
- Minced garlic, one teaspoon

Instructions:

1. In a large sauce pan, add the onions and oil.
2. Cook your onions and then add the ginger and garlic.
3. Cook your ginger and garlic and then add in the pork pieces.
4. Stir fry your pork pieces well.
5. Add all the spices and the rest of the ingredients into your dish except the basil leaves.
6. When your pork is cooked then add the basil leaves.
7. Cook your dish for five minutes.
8. Garnish your dish with cilantro.
9. Your dish is ready to be served.

4.8 Thai Green Chicken Curry with Vegetables Recipe

Preparation Time: 30 minutes

Cooking Time: 10 minutes

Serving: 4

Ingredients:

- Galangal, one can
- Chicken stock, two cups
- Minced garlic, one teaspoon
- Shallot, one
- Kaffir lime leaves, four
- Lime wedges
- Lemon grass, two sticks
- Fish sauce, two tablespoon
- Thai green curry paste, two tablespoon
- Mixed vegetables, one cup
- Cilantro, a quarter cup
- Chicken pieces, half pound
- Olive oil, one tablespoon

Instructions:

1. Take a large sauce pan.

2. Add the shallots and olive oil.

3. Cook your shallots and then add the chicken pieces and vegetables.

4. When the chicken pieces are half cooked, add the galangal, green curry paste, chicken stock, and minced garlic.

5. Cook your ingredients until it starts boiling.

6. Add in the lemon grass and rest of the ingredients into your soup.

7. Cook your ingredients for ten minutes.

8. When your chicken pieces are cooked completely dish out your soup.

9. Garnish it with cilantro leaves.

10. Your dish is ready to be served.

4.9 Thai Mussels in Basil Coconut Sauce Recipe

Preparation Time: 30 minutes

Cooking Time: 10 minutes

Serving: 4

Ingredients:

- Galangal, one can
- Fish stock, two cups

- Minced garlic, one teaspoon
- Minced ginger, one teaspoon
- Chopped onion, half cup
- Crushed ginger, half tablespoon
- Basil leaves, a quarter cup
- Fish sauce, two tablespoon
- Shredded coconut, one cup
- Coconut milk, one cup
- Cilantro, a quarter cup
- Mussels, half pound
- Olive oil, one tablespoon

Instructions:
1. Take a large sauce pan.
2. Add the chopped onion and olive oil.
3. Cook your chopped onion and then add the mussels.
4. When the mussels are half cooked then add the galangal, fish stock, minced garlic and ginger.
5. Add the coconut milk.
6. Cook your ingredients until it starts boiling.
7. Add in the shredded coconut, basil leaves and rest of the ingredients into your curry.
8. Cook your ingredients for ten minutes.
9. Garnish it with cilantro leaves.
10. Your dish is ready to be served.

4.10 Thai Pumpkin and Sweet Potato Curry Recipe

Preparation Time: 30 minutes

Cooking Time: 10 minutes

Serving: 4

Ingredients:

- Galangal, one can
- Chicken stock, two cups
- Chopped garlic, one teaspoon
- Palm sugar, two tablespoon
- Shallot, one
- Lemon grass, two sticks
- Fish sauce, two tablespoon
- Sweet potatoes, one cup
- Coconut milk, one cup
- Cilantro, a quarter cup
- Pumpkin pieces, two cups
- Olive oil, one tablespoon

Instructions:

1. Take a large sauce pan.

2. Add the shallots and olive oil.

3. Cook your shallots.

4. When the pumpkin and sweet potatoes is half cooked, add the galangal, chicken stock, and minced garlic.

5. Cook your ingredients until it starts boiling.

6. Add in the lemon grass and rest of the ingredients into your curry.

7. Cook your ingredients for ten minutes.

8. Garnish it with cilantro leaves.

9. Your dish is ready to be served.

4.11 Thai Tofu Fried Rice Recipe

Preparation Time: 30 minutes

Cooking Time: 10 minutes

Serving: 4

Ingredients:

- Tofu cubes, one cup
- Jalapeno, one large
- Sliced green onions, half cup
- White peppercorns, one teaspoon
- Cilantro, one cup
- Fresh ginger, one teaspoon
- Fish sauce, one tablespoon
- Soy sauce, one tablespoon

- Chinese 5 spice, half teaspoon
- Chili garlic sauce, two tablespoon
- Fresh cilantro leaves, half cup
- Thai basil leaves, a quarter cup
- Vegetable broth, one can
- Minced lemon grass, one teaspoon
- Cooked rice, as required

Instructions:

1. Add all the ingredients of the curry into a pan.
2. Add the vegetable broth and sauces into the mixture.
3. Cook your dish for ten minutes.
4. Add the cooked rice into the mixture once the curry is ready.
5. Mix the rice well and cook it for five minutes.
6. Add the tofu pieces into the pan by pushing the rest of the ingredients to a side.
7. Cook the tofu pieces and then mix the rest of the ingredients into it.
8. Cook your dish for five more minutes.
9. Add the cilantro into the dish.
10. Mix your rice and then dish it out.
11. Your dish is ready to be served.

4.12 Thai Chicken Pad Thai Recipe

Preparation Time: 30 minutes

Cooking Time: 10 minutes

Serving: 4

Ingredients:

- Mixed vegetables, two cups
- Sliced green onions, half cup
- White peppercorns, one teaspoon
- Cilantro, one cup
- Fresh ginger, one teaspoon
- Fish sauce, one tablespoon
- Soy sauce, one tablespoon
- Chinese 5 spice, half teaspoon
- Chili garlic sauce, two tablespoon
- Fresh cilantro leaves, half cup
- Thai basil leaves, a quarter cup
- Chicken broth, one can
- Chicken pieces, half pound
- Cooked noodles, as required

Instructions:

1. Add all the ingredients of the sauce into a pan.
2. Add the chicken pieces, vegetables, chicken broth and sauces into the mixture.
3. Cook your dish for ten minutes.
4. Add the cooked noodles into the mixture once the sauce is ready.
5. Mix the noodles well and cook it for five minutes.
6. Add the cilantro into the dish.
7. Mix your noodles and then dish it out.
8. Your dish is ready to be served.

4.13 Thai Sour and Spicy Soup Recipe

Preparation Time: 30 minutes

Cooking Time: 10 minutes

Serving: 4

Ingredients:

- Galangal, one can
- Vegetables stock, two cups
- Minced garlic, one teaspoon
- Palm sugar, two tablespoon
- Shallot, one
- Sweet and sour sauce, half cup
- Ginger pieces, a quarter cup

- Lemon grass, two sticks
- Fish sauce, two tablespoon
- Mixed vegetables, one cup
- Coconut milk, one cup
- Cilantro, a quarter cup
- Olive oil, one tablespoon

Instructions:

1. Take a large sauce pan.
2. Add the shallots and olive oil.
3. Cook your shallots and then add the mixed vegetables.
4. When the vegetables are cooked then add the galangal, vegetable stock, and minced garlic.
5. Add the ginger pieces and coconut milk.
6. Cook your ingredients until it starts boiling.
7. Add in the sweet and sour sauce, lemon grass and rest of the ingredients into your soup.
8. Cook your ingredients for ten minutes.
9. Garnish it with cilantro leaves.
10. Your dish is ready to be served.

4.14 Thai Pumpkin and Coconut Curry Recipe

Preparation Time: 30 minutes

Cooking Time: 10 minutes

Serving: 4

Ingredients:

- Galangal, one can
- Vegetable stock, two cups
- Minced garlic, one teaspoon
- Minced ginger, one teaspoon
- Chopped onion, half cup
- Minced ginger, half tablespoon
- Lemon grass, two sticks
- Fish sauce, two tablespoon
- Shredded coconut, one cup
- Coconut milk, one cup
- Cilantro, a quarter cup
- Pumpkin pieces, half pound
- Olive oil, one tablespoon

Instructions:

1. Take a large sauce pan.
2. Add the chopped onion and olive oil.
3. Cook your chopped onion and then add the pumpkin pieces.
4. When the pumpkin pieces are half cooked then add the galangal, vegetable stock, minced garlic and ginger.

5. Add the coconut milk.

6. Add in the shredded coconut, lemon grass and rest of the ingredients into your curry.

7. Cook your ingredients for ten minutes.

8. Garnish it with cilantro leaves.

9. Your dish is ready to be served.

4.15 Thai Grilled Salmon Recipe

Preparation Time: 30 minutes

Cooking Time: 25 minutes

Serving: 4

Ingredients:

- Minced ginger, two tablespoon
- Cilantro, half cup
- Olive oil, two tablespoon
- Chopped tomatoes, one cup
- Powdered cumin, one tablespoon
- Salt, to taste
- Black pepper, to taste
- Turmeric powder, one teaspoon
- Fresh Thai herbs, two tablespoon
- Onion, one cup
- Salmon filet, one pound

- Minced garlic, two tablespoon

Instructions:

1. Take a pan.
2. Add in the oil and onions.
3. Cook the onions until they become soft and fragrant.
4. Add in the chopped garlic and ginger.
5. Cook the mixture and add the tomatoes into it.
6. Add the spices.
7. Mix the salmon so that the tomatoes and spices are coated all over the salmon.
8. Place fresh Thai herbs on the salmon.
9. Grill your salmon for fifteen to twenty minutes.
10. When your salmon is done, dish it out.
11. Sprinkle the cilantro on top of the salmon.
12. Your dish is ready to be served.

4.16 Thai Red Beef Curry Recipe

Preparation Time: 30 minutes

Cooking Time: 10 minutes

Serving: 4

Ingredients:

- Beef stock, two cups
- Crushed garlic, one teaspoon

- Palm sugar, two tablespoon
- Shallot, one
- Kaffir lime leaves, four
- Lemon grass, two sticks
- Fish sauce, two tablespoon
- Thai red curry paste, two tablespoon
- Cilantro, a quarter cup
- Beef, half pound
- Olive oil, one tablespoon

Instructions:
1. Take a large sauce pan.
2. Add the shallots and olive oil.
3. Cook your shallots and then add the beef meat.
4. When the beef is half cooked, add the red curry paste, beef stock, and minced garlic.
5. Cook your ingredients until it starts boiling.
6. Add in the lemon grass and rest of the ingredients into the curry.
7. Cook your ingredients for ten minutes.
8. When your curry is cooked, dish it out.
9. Garnish it with cilantro leaves.
10.   Your dish is ready to be served.

4.17 Thai Coconut Curry Recipe

Preparation Time: 30 minutes

Cooking Time: 10 minutes

Serving: 4

Ingredients:

- Galangal, one can
- Vegetable stock, two cups
- Minced garlic, one teaspoon
- Minced ginger, one teaspoon
- Chopped onion, half cup
- Chopped ginger, half tablespoon
- Lemon grass, two sticks
- Fish sauce, two tablespoon
- Shredded coconut, one cup
- Coconut milk, one cup
- Cilantro, a quarter cup
- Olive oil, one tablespoon

Instructions:

1. Take a large sauce pan.
2. Add the chopped onion and olive oil.
3. Cook your chopped onion.

4. When the onions are cooked then add the galangal, vegetable stock, minced garlic and ginger.

5. Add the coconut milk.

6. Cook your ingredients until it starts boiling.

7. Add in the shredded coconut, lemon grass and rest of the ingredients into your curry.

8. Cook your ingredients for ten minutes.

9. Garnish it with cilantro leaves.

10. Your dish is ready to be served.

4.18 Thai Pumpkin and Vegetable Soup Recipe

Preparation Time: 30 minutes

Cooking Time: 10 minutes

Serving: 4

Ingredients:

- Vegetables stock, two cups
- Minced garlic, one teaspoon
- Galangal, one can
- Shallot, one
- Pumpkin pieces, one cup
- Ginger pieces, a quarter cup
- Lemon grass, two sticks
- Fish sauce, two tablespoon

- Mixed vegetables, one cup
- Coconut milk, one cup
- Cilantro, a quarter cup
- Olive oil, one tablespoon

Instructions:
1. Take a large sauce pan.
2. Add the shallots and olive oil.
3. Cook your shallots and then add the mixed vegetables.
4. When the vegetables are cooked then add the galangal, vegetable stock, and minced garlic.
5. Add the ginger pieces and coconut milk.
6. Cook your ingredients until it starts boiling.
7. Add in the pumpkin, lemon grass and rest of the ingredients into your soup.
8. Cook your ingredients for ten minutes.
9. Garnish it with cilantro leaves.
10. Your dish is ready to be served.

Chapter 5: The World of Traditional Thai Dessert Recipes

Following are some classic traditional Thai dessert recipes that are rich in healthy nutrients and you can easily make them with the detailed instructions list in each recipe:

5.1 Thai Coconut Pudding Recipe

Preparation Time: 10 minutes

Cooking Time: 30 minutes

Serving: 2

Ingredients:
- Coconut Milk, two cups
- White sugar, half cup
- Salt, one teaspoon
- Eggs, two
- Lemon extract, one teaspoon
- Almond extract, one teaspoon
- All-purpose flour, two cups
- Butter, one cup
- Dry yeast, one cup

Instructions:

1. Take a medium bowl and add the butter in it.
2. Add one cup flour and mix well.
3. Then refrigerate it.
4. Take a large bowl and add yeast into it.
5. Add the sugar, the salt and the milk.
6. Mix them well.
7. Mix the warm milk mixture with the flour and the yeast.
8. Add the lemon extract, eggs and almond extract together.
9. Add the baking soda in the mixture.
10. Simmer it for few minutes.
11. Check the thickness of the pudding.
12. Serve warm.

5.2 Thai Fruit Salad Recipe

Preparation Time: 10 minutes

Cooking Time: 30 minutes

Serving: 2

Ingredients:

- Bananas, five or six
- Apples, two or three
- Spring onions, three
- Gem lettuce, separated into leaves

- Lime zest, one
- Chili sauce, one teaspoon
- Fish sauce, one tablespoon
- Rice vinegar, one tablespoon
- Sugar, one tablespoon
- Sesame oil, one tablespoon
- Sesame seeds, one cup

Instructions:

1. Take a large bowl to put all the ingredients into it.
2. First of all, slice the bananas into small pieces so that proper mixing can be done.
3. Then slice the apples in the same way.
4. Put them into the bowl.
5. Add chili sauce and fish sauce into the bowl.
6. Add all spices one by one.
7. Add the rice vinegar in such a way equal distribution can be done.
8. Take the gem lettuce in a separate bowl.
9. Add the lime zest and juice into it.
10. Add the spring onions, sesame seeds and sesame oil into it.
11. Mix all the ingredients so that a good paste is formed
12. Then add it in the first bowl with apples and bananas.
13. You can add sugar as per your requirement.

14. Your salad is ready to be served with chili sauce.

5.3 Thai Mung Bean Pudding Recipe

Preparation Time: 10 minutes

Cooking Time: 15 minutes

Serving: 4

Ingredients:

- Tapioca flour, one cup
- Mung beans, half cup
- Coconut milk, half cup
- White sugar, half cup
- Salt, one teaspoon
- Eggs, two
- Lemon extract, one teaspoon
- Almond extract, one teaspoon
- All-purpose flour, two cups
- Butter, one cup

Instructions:

1. Take a medium bowl and add the mung beans in it.
2. Add one cup tapioca flour and mix well.
3. Then refrigerate it.

4. Take a large bowl and add the coconut milk into it.

5. Add the sugar, salt and milk.

6. Mix them well.

7. Mix the warm milk mixture with the flour and the mung beans.

8. Add the eggs, lemon extract and almond extract together.

9. Add the baking soda in the mixture.

10. Simmer it for few minutes.

11. Check the thickness of the pudding.

12. Your dish is ready to be served.

5.4 Thai Mango Sticky Rice Recipe

Preparation Time: 10 minutes

Cooking Time: 10 minutes

Serving: 4

Ingredients:

- Water, one and a half cup
- Ripe mangoes, two
- Thai sweet rice, one cup
- Coconut milk, one can
- Salt, a quarter teaspoon
- Brown sugar, five tablespoon

Instructions:

1. Add half cup of water, rice, plus half can of the coconut milk, the salt, and one tablespoon of the brown sugar.

2. Stir well.

3. Add coconut milk, salt, and some of the brown sugar to the saucepan.

4. Bring to a gentle boil, and then partially cover with a lid.

5. Reduce heat to medium-low, or just until you get a gentle simmer.

6. Simmer thirty minutes, or until the coconut water has been absorbed by the rice.

7. Turn off the heat but leave the pot on the burner with the lid on it tightly.

8. Allow it to stay for five minutes.

9. To make the sauce, warm the remaining coconut milk over medium-low heat.

10. Add three tablespoons of brown sugar, stirring to dissolve.

11. Prepare the mangoes by cutting them open and slicing each into bite-sized pieces.

12. Scoop some warm rice into each serving bowl, and then drizzle lots of the sweet coconut sauce over the top.

13. Arrange mango slices on the rice and finish with a drizzle of more sauce.

14. Your dish is ready to be served.

5.5 Thai Mango Tapioca Pudding Recipe

Preparation Time: 10 minutes

Cooking Time: 10 minutes

Serving: 4

Ingredients:

- Tapioca flour, one cup
- Mangoes, two
- Coconut milk, half cup
- White sugar, half cup
- Salt, one teaspoon
- Eggs, two
- Lemon extract, one teaspoon
- Almond extract, one teaspoon
- All-purpose flour, two cups
- Butter, one cup

Instructions:

1. Take a medium bowl and add the tapioca flour in it.
2. Add the one cup coconut milk and mix well.
3. Then refrigerate it.

4. Take a large bowl and add the spices into it.

5. Add the sugar, salt and mangoes.

6. Mix them well.

7. Mix the warm milk mixture with the flour and the mangoes.

8. Add the eggs, lemon extract and almond extract together.

9. Add the baking soda in the mixture.

10. Simmer it for few minutes.

11. Check the thickness of the pudding.

12. Your dish is ready to be served.

5.6 Thai Fried Bananas Recipe

Preparation Time: 30 minutes

Cooking Time: 10 minutes

Serving: 4

Ingredients:

- Bananas, five
- Cornstarch, one tablespoon
- Water, two cups
- Coconut milk, one cup
- Rice flour, one cup
- Chinese five spice, as needed
- Cooking oil, as required

Instructions:

1. In a large bowl, add all the ingredients together except the bananas and oil.
2. Mix everything to form a consistent mixture.
3. Dip your bananas into the mixture and then fry them in the cooking oil.
4. Fry your bananas until they turn golden brown.
5. Dish out and drizzle maple syrup if you want on top.
6. Your dish is ready to be served.

5.7 Thai Steamed Banana Cake Recipe

Preparation Time: 10 minutes

Cooking Time: 20 minutes

Serving: 4

Ingredients:

- Bananas, five
- Salt, two tablespoon
- White sugar, two cups
- Cornstarch, one tablespoon
- Water, two cups
- Coconut milk, one cup
- Rice flour, one cup
- Pandan essence, as needed

- Raspberries, aa required

Instructions:
1. Take bananas and peel them.
2. Then steam them properly.
3. Take water in a pot and heat it.
4. Take a large bowl and add the sweet rice into it.
5. Cook the rice and add some of sugar into it for taste.
6. Take another bowl and add coconut milk into it.
7. Mix the palm sugar into the coconut milk.
8. Then mix the rice cooked and coconut milk together.
9. Take them into a large bowl after mixing.
10. Add steamed bananas and raspberries into it.
11. Mix them well and then bake your cake.
12. Your cake is ready to be served.

5.8 Thai Tea Cake Recipe

Preparation Time: 10 minutes

Cooking Time: 40 minutes

Serving: 2

Ingredients:

- Tea, one cup
- Salt, two tablespoon
- White sugar, two cups
- Cornstarch, one tablespoon
- Water, two cups
- Coconut milk, one cup
- Rice flour, one cup
- Pandan essence, as needed
- Raspberries, as required

Instructions:
1. Take one cup of tea.
2. Take water in a pot and heat it.
3. Take a large bowl and add the sweet rice into it.
4. Cook the rice and add some of the sugar into it for taste.
5. Take another bowl and add coconut milk into it.
6. Mix the palm sugar into the coconut milk.
7. Then mix the rice cooked and coconut milk together.
8. Take them into a large bowl after mixing.
9. Mix them well and then bake your cake.
10. Your cake is ready to be served.

5.9 Thai Banana Spring Rolls Recipe

Preparation Time: 10 minutes

Cooking Time: 10 minutes

Serving: 2

Ingredients:

- Chopped bananas, five
- Shredded coconut, half cup
- Wonton wraps, as required
- Chinese five spice, as needed
- Cooking oil, as required

Instructions:

1. In a large bowl, mix all the ingredients together.
2. Add the mixture into the wonton wrappers.
3. Wrap your rolls.
4. Fry your rolls until they turn golden brown.
5. Dish out and drizzle any sauce if you want on top.
6. Your dish is ready to be served.

5.10 Thai Mango Cake Recipe

Preparation Time: 30 minutes

Cooking Time: 10 minutes

Serving: 4

Ingredients:

- Mangoes, three
- Salt, two tablespoon
- White sugar, two cups
- Cornstarch, one tablespoon
- Water, two cups
- Coconut milk, one cup
- Rice flour, one cup
- Raspberries, aa required

Instructions:

1. Take the mangoes into a bowl.
2. Slice them into small pieces.
3. Add salt to it for taste as required.
4. Take water in a pot and heat it.
5. Take a large bowl and add the sweet rice into it.
6. Cook the rice and add some of the sugar into it for taste.
7. Take another bowl and add coconut milk into it.
8. Mix the palm sugar into the coconut milk.
9. Then mix the sliced mangoes and coconut milk together.

10.   Take them into a large bowl after mixing.

11.   Add the coconut juice and raspberries into it.

12.   Mix them well.

13.   Then bake them for fifteen minutes.

14.   After cooking, you can refrigerate the cake.

15.   Your cake is ready to be served.

5.11 Thai Coconut Cake Recipe

Preparation Time: 10 minutes

Cooking Time: 10 minutes

Serving: 4

Ingredients:

- Coconut, two
- Salt, two tablespoon
- White sugar, two cups
- Cornstarch, one tablespoon
- Water, two cups
- Coconut milk, one cup
- Rice flour, one cup
- Raspberries, aa required

Instructions:

1. Take the coconut juice into a bowl.
2. Add salt to it for taste as required.
3. Take water in a pot and heat it.
4. Take a large bowl and add the sweet rice into it.
5. Cook the rice and add some of sugar into it for taste.

6. Take another bowl and add coconut milk into it.

7. Mix the palm sugar into the coconut milk.

8. Then mix the rice cooked and coconut milk together.

9. Take them into a large bowl after mixing.

10. Add the coconut juice and raspberries into it.

11. Mix them well.

12. Then bake them for fifteen minutes.

13. After cooking you can refrigerate the cake.

14. Your cake is ready to be served.

5.12 Thai Mango Ice Cream Recipe

Preparation Time: 10 minutes

Cooking Time: 15 minutes

Serving: 2

- Mangoes, two
- Coconut milk, half cup
- White sugar, half cup
- Salt, one teaspoon
- Eggs, two
- Lemon extract, one teaspoon
- Almond extract, one teaspoon
- All-purpose flour, two cups

- Butter, one cup

Instructions:

1. Slice the mangoes into small pieces.
2. Take a medium bowl and add the tapioca flour in it.
3. Add one cup of coconut milk and mix well.
4. Then refrigerate it.
5. Take a large bowl and add the spices into it.
6. Add the sugar, the salt and the spices.
7. Mix them well.
8. Mix the warm milk mixture with the flour and the sliced mangoes.
9. Add the eggs, the lemon extract and the almond extract together.
10. Add the baking soda in the mixture.
11. Simmer it for few minutes.
12. Check the thickness of the ice cream.
13. Refrigerate it.
14. Your dish is ready to be served.

5.13 Thai Sticky Black Rice Pudding Recipe

Preparation Time: 15 minutes

Cooking Time: 25 minutes

Serving: 3

Ingredients:

- Black rice, two cups
- Chinese sweet spices, to taste
- Coconut milk, half cup
- White sugar, half cup
- Salt, one teaspoon
- Eggs, two
- Lemon extract, one teaspoon
- Almond extract, one teaspoon
- All-purpose flour, two cups
- Butter, one cup

Instructions:

1. Cook the black rice in the rice cooking pan.
2. Take a medium bowl and add the tapioca flour in it.
3. Add one cup of coconut milk and mix well.
4. Then refrigerate it.
5. Take a large bowl and add the spices into it.
6. Add the sugar, the salt and the spices.
7. Mix them well.
8. Mix the warm milk mixture with the flour and the cooked rice.
9. Add the eggs, lemon extract and almond extract together.

10. Add the baking soda in the mixture.

11. Simmer it for few minutes.

12. Your dish is ready to be served.

5.14 Thai Egg and Coconut Custard Recipe

Preparation Time: 30 minutes

Cooking Time: 10 minutes

Serving: 4

Ingredients:

- Eggs, two
- Coconut, two
- Chinese sweet spices, to taste
- Coconut milk, half cup
- White sugar, half cup
- Salt, one teaspoon
- Lemon extract, one teaspoon
- Almond extract, one teaspoon
- All-purpose flour, two cups
- Butter, one cup

Instructions:

1. Take a medium bowl and add the eggs and the tapioca flour in it.
2. Add one cup of coconut milk and mix well.

3. Then refrigerate it.

4. Take a large bowl and add the spices into it.

5. Add the sugar, the salt and the beaten eggs.

6. Mix them well.

7. Mix the warm milk mixture with the flour and coconut.

8. Add the eggs, lemon extract and almond extract together.

9. Add the baking soda in the mixture.

10. Simmer it for few minutes.

11. Check the thickness of the custard.

12. Your dish is ready to be served.

5.15 Thai Sweet Corn Pudding Recipe

Preparation Time: 10 minutes

Cooking Time: 30 minutes

Serving: 4

Ingredients:

- Butter, one cup
- Sweet corn, one cup
- Eggs, two
- Cherries, two
- All-purpose flour, two cups
- Water, as required

- Baking soda, one tablespoon
- Salt, a pinch
- Walnuts, one cup

Instructions:
1. Take a large bowl and clean it well.
2. Add the sweet corn and the baking soda.
3. Add the salt and the cream.
4. Mix all the ingredients well.
5. Add beaten eggs into the mixture.
6. Pour into the dish and spread evenly.
7. Take a small bowl and add the sugar and the butter.
8. Mix them until it becomes smooth.
9. Add the mixture into flour and mix well.
10. Simmer it for about twenty-five minutes
11. Your dish is ready to be served.

Chapter 6: The World of Traditional Thai Recipes Eaten Only by Thai People

Following are some classic traditional Thai recipes eaten only by Thai people that are rich in healthy nutrients and you can easily make them with the detailed instructions list given in each recipe:

6.1 Patonga (Thai Breakfast Donut) Recipe

Preparation Time: 15 minutes

Cooking Time: 30 minutes

Serving: 3

Ingredients:

- All-purpose flour, one cup
- Baking soda, one cup
- Sugar, two tablespoon
- Water, half cup
- Vegetable oil, two cups
- Milk, two cups
- Walnuts, one cup
- Eggs, four
- Cherries, one cup
- Butter as needed

Instructions:

1. Take a large bowl and clean it well.
2. Add the sugar and the baking soda.
3. Add the salt and the cream.
4. Mix all the ingredients well.
5. Add beaten eggs into the mixture.
6. Pour into the dish and spread evenly.
7. Take a small bowl and add the sugar and the butter.
8. Mix them until become smooth.
9. Add the mixture into flour and mix well.
10. Bake it for about twenty-five minutes.
11. Your dish is ready to be served.

6.2 Khanom Kharuk (Thai Mini Pancakes) Recipe

Preparation Time: 30 minutes

Cooking Time: 50 minutes

Serving: 5

Ingredients:

- Blackberry jam, one cup
- Butter, one cup
- Eggs, two
- Cherries, two

- All-purpose flour, two cups
- Water, as required
- Baking soda, one tablespoon
- Salt, a pinch
- Walnuts, one cup

Instructions:

1. Take a large bowl and clean it well.
2. Add the sugar and the baking soda.
3. Add the salt and the cream.
4. Mix all the ingredients well.
5. Add beaten eggs into the mixture.
6. Add blackberry jam into it.
7. Pour into the dish and spread evenly.
8. Take a small bowl and add the sugar and the butter.
9. Mix them until the mixture becomes smooth.
10. Add the mixture into flour and mix well.
11. Bake it for about thirty-five minutes.
12. Your dish is ready to be served.

6.3 Jauk (The Rice Porridge) Recipe

Preparation Time: 20 minutes

Cooking Time: 20 minutes

Serving: 2

Ingredients:

- Fish sauce, three teaspoon
- Brown cooked rice, two cups
- Ground pork, one cup
- Cilantro, one tablespoon
- Black pepper, to taste
- Chicken broth, four cups
- Egg white, half cup
- Galangal, one slice
- Ginger, two tablespoon
- Palm sugar, one tablespoon
- Lime juice, one tablespoon
- Alfa one rice bran oil, teaspoon
- Coconut milk, one cup
- Bean sprouts, one cup
- Fried shallots, to serve
- Red chili, to serve

Instructions:

1. Cook the rice in rice cooker.
2. Then refrigerate it.
3. Prepare meat balls by mixing all the ingredients one by one
4. Cook it for one minute with continuous stirring.

5. Add the coconut milk into the mixture.

6. Boil the coconut milk along with mixture.

7. Continue boiling for five minutes until water reduces to minimum level.

8. Add the egg whites and mix well.

9. Then take the chicken broth in a separate large pot.

10.   Add the lemon grass and galangal in it.

11.   Simmer it for five minutes.

12.   Then add them in already cooked brown rice.

13.   Adjust taste by adding pepper and salt.

14.   Your soup is ready to be served.

15.   Serve it with chilies and soy sauce.

6.4 Khao Tom (The Rice Porridge Soup) Recipe

Preparation Time: 10 minutes

Cooking Time: 25 minutes

Serving: 3

Ingredients:

- Fish sauce, three teaspoon
- Brown cooked rice, two cups
- Ground pork, one cup

- Cilantro, one tablespoon
- Black pepper, to taste
- Chicken broth, four cups
- Egg white, half cup
- Galangal, one slice
- Ginger, two tablespoon
- Palm sugar, one tablespoon
- Lime juice, one tablespoon
- Alfa one rice bran oil, teaspoon
- Coconut milk, one cup
- Bean sprouts, one cup
- Fried shallots, to serve
- Red chili, to serve

Instructions:
1. Cook the rice in rice cooker.
2. Then refrigerate it.
3. Prepare meat balls by mixing all the ingredients one by one
4. Cook it for one minute with continuous stirring.
5. Add the coconut milk into the mixture.
6. Boil the coconut milk along with mixture.
7. Continue boiling for five minutes until water reduces to minimum level.
8. Add the egg white and mix well.
9. Then take the chicken broth in separate large pot.

10.   Add the lemon grass and galangal in it.

11.   Simmer it for five minutes.

12.   Then add them in already cooked brown rice.

13.   Adjust taste by adding pepper and salt.

14.   Your soup is ready to be served.

15.   Serve it with chilies and soy sauce.

6.5 Dim Sum (Thai Steamed Buns) Recipe

Preparation Time: 50 minutes

Cooking Time: 30 minutes

Serving: 4

Ingredients:

- Ground pork, half pound
- Thin soy sauce, one tablespoon
- Thai pepper powder, half tablespoon
- Sugar, one tablespoon
- Garlic powder, one tablespoon
- Fresh shallot, half tablespoon
- Milk, one cup
- Vegetable oil, one tablespoon
- All-purpose flour, one cup
- Whole wheat flour, half cup

- Salt, to taste
- Water, to kneed
- Cucumber, one
- Yeast, one cup

Instructions:

1. Take a bowl and add the flour into it.
2. Then add the yeast and sugar into it.
3. Add lukewarm water in it.
4. Set aside for half an hour.
5. In another bowl, take the whole wheat flour.
6. Add the yeast dough in it.
7. Then add the salt and some water in it.
8. Then combine the ingredients to form a soft dough.
9. Kneed it for ten minutes.
10. Meanwhile, chop all the vegetables.
11. Mix them with soy sauce, chili vinegar, sugar and salt.
12. Make round forms of dough with the help of the oil.
13. Then bake your buns for ten minutes.
14. Once the buns are steamed, take them out.
15. You can serve Thai buns with salad.

6.6 Thai Sweet Rice Cakes Recipe

Preparation Time: 2 minutes

Cooking Time: 25 minutes

Serving: 2

Ingredients:

- Thai sweet rice, two cups
- Salt, two tablespoon
- White sugar, two cups
- Cornstarch, one tablespoon
- Water, two cups
- Coconut milk, one cup
- Rice flour, one cup
- Pandan essence, as needed
- Raspberries, aa required

Instructions:
1. Take a blender and blend the pandan leaves.
2. Then add the paste type material into a bowl.
3. Press the paste so that all juice comes out.
4. Take the juice and discard the solids.
5. Take water in a pot and heat it.
6. Take a large bowl and add the sweet rice into it.

7. Cook the rice and add some of the sugar into it for taste.

8. Take another bowl and add coconut milk into it.

9. Mix the palm sugar into the coconut milk.

10. Then mix the cooked rice and coconut milk together.

11. Take them into a large bowl after mixing.

12. Add pandan juice and raspberries into it.

13. Mix them well.

14. Then bake them well.

15. After cooking you can refrigerate the cake.

16. Your cake is ready to be served.

6.7 Thai Steamed Pandan Cakes Recipe

Preparation Time: 15 minutes

Cooking Time: 35 minutes

Serving: 2

Ingredients:

- Pandan leaves, one bunch
- Tapioca starch, one cup
- Arrowroot starch, one cup
- Water, two cups
- Coconut milk, one cup

- Rice flour, one cup
- Jasmine tea, one cup

Instructions:

1. Take a blender and blend the pandan leaves.
2. Then add the paste type material into a bowl.
3. Press the paste so that all juice comes out.
4. Take the juice and discard the solids.
5. Take water in a pot and heat it.
6. Take a large bowl and add rice flour into it.
7. Then whisk it with tapioca starch and arrowroot starch.
8. Take another bowl and add coconut milk into it.
9. Mix the palm sugar into the coconut milk.
10. Then mix the rice flour and coconut milk together.
11. Take them into a large bowl after mixing.
12. Add pandan juice and jasmine tea into it.
13. Mix them well and cook them efficiently.
14. After cooking you can refrigerate the whole food.
15. Your cake is ready to be served.

6.8 Thai Carrot and Radish Salad Recipe

Preparation Time: 5 minutes

Cooking Time: 5 minutes

Serving: 3

Ingredients:

- Carrots, two
- Radishes, ten
- Spring onions, three
- Gem lettuce, separated into leaves
- Lime zest, one
- Chili sauce, one teaspoon
- Fish sauce, one tablespoon
- Rice vinegar, one tablespoon
- Sugar, one tablespoon
- Sesame oil, one tablespoon
- Sesame seeds, one cup

Instructions:

1. Take a large bowl to put all the ingredients into it.
2. First of all, slice the carrots into small pieces so that proper mixing can be done.

3. Then slice the radish in the same way.

4. Put them into the bowl.

5. Add chili sauce and fish sauce into the bowl.

6. Add all spices one by one.

7. Add the rice vinegar in such a way that equal distribution can be done.

8. Take the gem lettuce in a separate bowl.

9. Add the lime zest and juice into it.

10. Add the spring onions, sesame seeds and sesame oil into it.

11. Mix all the ingredients so that a good paste is formed

12. Then add it in the first bowl with carrots and radishes.

13. You can add sugar as per your requirement.

14. Your salad is ready to be served with chili sauce.

6.9 Thai Fish Broth with Vegetables Recipe

Preparation Time: 10 minutes

Cooking Time: 25 minutes

Serving: 4

Ingredients:

- Brown rice noodles, one cup
- Chicken, two cups

- Red curry paste, one teaspoon
- Fish sauce, one tablespoon
- White fish, one bowl
- Red chili, to serve
- Prawns, one cup
- Fried shallots, to serve
- Salt, to taste
- Pepper, to taste
- Lime leaves, one cup

Instructions:
1. Take a large saucepan and add oil in it.
2. Heat it over medium high heat.
3. Add the brown rice noodles into it.
4. Cook it for one minute with the continuous stirring.
5. Add the chicken into the mixture.
6. Boil the chicken and curry paste along with mixture.
7. Continue boiling for five minutes until water reduces to minimum level.
8. Add the lime leaves in a separate bowl.
9. And cover it with the boiling water for five minutes.
10. Add fish into the mixture and boil until the meat becomes soft and tender.

11.   Add the fish sauce, lime juice and peas into the mixture.

12.   Add the prawns to the mixture in the end having all the ingredients.

13.   Cook for five minutes so that color and texture of the fish become suitable.

14.   Your dish is ready to be served with the sauces and spices you want.

6.10 Thai Prawn and Coconut Soup Recipe

Preparation Time: 10 minutes

Cooking Time: 25 minutes

Serving: 2

Ingredients:

- sauce, three teaspoon
- Palm sugar, one tablespoon
- Lime juice, one tablespoon
- Peas, trimmed, one cup
- Peeled prawns, two cups
- Alfa one rice bran oil, teaspoon
- Coconut milk, one cup
- Bean sprouts, one cup
- Fried shallots, to serve

- Red chili, to serve
- Red curry paste, half cup
- Noodles, one packet

Instructions:

1. Take a large saucepan and add oil in it.
2. Heat it over medium high heat.
3. Add curry paste into it.
4. Cook it for one minute with continuous stirring.
5. Add the coconut milk into the mixture.
6. Boil the coconut milk along with mixture.
7. Continue boiling for five minutes until water reduces to minimum level.
8. Add the noodles in a separate bowl.
9. Cover it with the boiling water for five minutes.
10. Then remove the noodles with the help of fork and drain it.
11. Add the fish sauce, lime juice and peas into the mixture.
12. Add the prawns to the soup.
13. Cook for five minutes.
14. Your soup is ready to be served.

Conclusion

While living a busy life, food becomes the one of the source of happiness for individuals in the 21st century. Different cuisines are available in the world and each of them being totally different from the other, adds delight to the people's lives. Thai cuisine covers dishes from Thailand and Thai foods which are extremely popular in the whole world.

In this book, we have discussed different aspects of Thai cuisine and not only the recipes. We discussed in detail the history and origin of Thai foods. The various spices used in Thai cooking have enormous amount of amazing properties that has such positive and healthy impact on our overall health. This cookbook includes 70 recipes that consist of breakfast, lunch, dinner, dessert, and the recipes that are only eaten by Thai people. You can easily make these recipes at home without supervision of any kind. So start cooking today and enjoy the Thai cuisine more than ever.

INDIAN

COOKBOOK

70 Easy Recipes for
Traditional Food from
India

Maki Blanc

The information herein is offered for informational purposes solely and is universal as so. The presentation of the information is without contract or any type of guarantee assurance.

The trademarks that are used are without any consent, and the publication of the trademark is without permission or backing by the trademark owner. All trademarks and brands within this book are for clarifying purposes only and are the owned by the owners themselves, not affiliated with this document.

Contents

Introduction

Seasoning blends, heady herbs, and bright colors prevail in Indian cuisine, aromatic and tasty. It also contains anti-inflammatory micronutrients in abundance. If Indian cuisine is unfamiliar to you, it can seem intimidating, but do not worry: these dishes describe in the book are surprisingly simple to prepare. Indeed, once you have had a few culinary triumphs, you might choose to create Indian-influenced dishes, a frequent part of your culinary range. Fragrant spices, which are a staple of Indian cuisine, are better when used fresh. You will save money by purchasing fresh spices in limited amounts from your nearest natural foods market's bulk section.

In terms of cuisine, India can be split into four distinct regions. Each area contains numerous nations, each with its distinct cuisine. Here is a quick rundown of North, East, South, and West Indian delicacies. Of course, it is important to keep in mind that no single explanation can encompass the vast array of Indian cuisine. It can take years of meticulous and really enjoyable gastronomic exploration to discover it.

Indian cuisine offers a wide variety of flavors, both strong and subtle, that is as diverse as the country itself. Weather and elevation, as well as culture and faith, both have an impact on the area. They describe a broad range of cuisines, which is unsurprising in a world with an estimated 885 million people and a land area of 1,226,596 square miles. Aside from herbs' prominent use, flatbreads and much larger milk products than anywhere in Asia are traditional culinary threads that run through local cuisines. Based on the region, baked goods are made from wheat, rice, or ground vegetables, while processed foods include milk, cream, yogurt, heavy cream, cream cheese, and cheese.

Religion has unquestionably had the greatest impact on Indian cuisine. Centuries of Hindu tradition and a deep conviction in reincarnation have culminated in some of the world's most delectable vegetarian food. Vegans rely on a variety of whole and split vegetables for nutrition. They have a wholesome, diverse diet combined with grain, supported by vegetables and milk products, and flavored to the full. Indian cuisine is similar to defining European cuisine in that it encompasses all at once.

"Indian Cookbook" is a complete recipe book based on all types of Indian dishes. It has four chapters with detailed knowledge of the introduction to Indian cuisine. Recipes from different regions of India are given in each chapter. These chapters are characterized into breakfast, appetizers, snacks, lunch, dinner, desserts, soups, salad, and India's most famous dishes. Try these dishes at your home and make your meals more like Indians.

Chapter 1: Introduction to Indian Cuisine

Food and drink are considered to nourish both the soul and the skin in India; food is central to spiritual development, pleasure, and happiness. The Indian kitchen differs greatly from north to eastern side to south, with western and southern Indian curries leading the way to vegan Indian food since most Western people recognize and enjoy it.

A cook's ingenuity and situations are the only limits to the richness of Indian cuisine. Each Indian chef, rest assured, would be a master of seasoning, handling each one separately before mixing them into different masalas (spice blends). Indians, like foreigners, are passionate about their cuisine. Three meals per day are normal, but certain areas of the country are so impoverished that they can only manage one. More than 500 million Indians, out of a total population of 1.2 billion, survive on less than $2.50 per day. However, whoever can enjoy their three primary meals and pack as many tiffins (snack foods) as they can into their everyday diet without sabotaging their hunger.

1.1 History of Indian Cuisine

Ayurveda, the ancient philosophy of life, fitness, and immortality, has influenced modern Indian culinary traditions. Foods are classified in Ayurveda based on their positive and negative forces and medicinal benefits. It is now the most commonly practiced treatment system in India, established by the Aryans in the second millennium BC. The fundamental theory of 'you are what you consume – you consume accordingly to what you are' is that you cannot sustain a balanced body by eating inappropriate food.

Much of this has not prevented fast-food franchises from establishing themselves in India's megacities like Mumbai, Delhi, and Calcutta. However, the ordinary Indian will still choose home-cooked food and a nearby ayurvedic practitioner to everything else. Moreover, although meat (except beef) is not specifically forbidden in Hinduism, a number of Indians are vegetarians due to the close connection between moral purity and veganism. Ahimsa (non-injury) is a Hindu and Jains ideology, but Buddhism has a much less humane perspective and is more concerned with intellectual development than animal health.

Such foods are considered pure and holy, and they can be used in temple rituals. The Hindu pantheon has a favorite dish; Krishna, for example, enjoys dairy goods, while Ganesha is often represented with a bowl of modak. Prasad is any meal that is first given to the deities and then exchanged with others.

1.2 History of Traditional Dishes of Indian Food

Indians are voracious consumers of home-cooked food or something done in the privacy of their own homes. The idea of dining in cafes and a posh Indian restaurant tradition has only been around for around fifty years. The Indian side of the road restaurants known as Dhaba is more like a lifestyle – an oasis for truckers, bus riders, and tourists going anywhere by the highway in India's vast, scenic, and often demanding landscape are as common as residence food. India's traditional dishes have roots in the Muslim-Indian era.

Indians are passionate about their food. Cooking is regarded as an art form, and moms often begin teaching their girls and passing down traditional foods by show-and-tell when their daughters are young. Mealtimes are significant moments for family gatherings. The majority of meals consist of many dishes ranging from basics such as rice and bread to meat and veg, followed by a dessert. Food is prepared from home with quality ingredients in many Indian families. Instead of buying grain from a supermarket, some families buy their favorite kind of grain, wash it, drying it in the heat, and then bring it to a factory to have it processed into flour just the way they like it! This is happening in larger cities, where people are happier to use ready-to-eat, pre-made foods because their lives are becoming more hectic.

1.3 Nutritional Information and Benefits of Indian Food

There are many benefits of Indian cuisine.
Chickpeas, for instance, which are frequently used in vegan curries, are high in fiber, calcium, riboflavin, and phosphorus, making them a nutritious addition to a vegan Indian diet. Superfoods such as broccoli and carrots, commonly used in Indian cuisine, produce rich antioxidants, nutrients, and minerals. Most Indian sauces and toppings, like Sag aloo and Gobhi Aloo (cabbage with vegetables), are veggies, making them a healthier option because they do not use milk or dairy. The tangy yogurt dipping raita, made with natural milk, tomato, and mint, is a low-fat option to sauces like mayonnaise and is a source of nutrients. In place of milk or cocoa powder, natural porridge is sometimes used to make curry preserves.

Garlic, which would be good for health, and cloves, which are great for the immune response and digestion, are commonly used in Indian cuisine. Instead of butter, Indian dishes frequently use grain, red pepper, and rice flour, maintaining the saturated fat content. Finally, since Indian dishes have such a strong flavor, a limited portion may also please taste buds while consuming fewer calories. The versatility and vibrancy of an Indian diet make it exciting, which is a good aspect of any cuisine because variety prevents repetition and overeating.

Finally, choosing tandoori recipes will reduce fat and calorie intake since they have very few sauces, and the meal, which is usually poultry and seafood, is grilled rather than fried.

Mango, bananas, pomegranates, figs, tomatoes, strawberries, grapefruit, oranges, and guavas are among the many delights of an Indian diet be consumed regularly to aid digestion and acquire minerals and vitamins.

1.4 Key ingredients of Indian Food

Here are some of the most important spices in Indian cooking.

Garam Masala: Garam means "hot" or "warm" in Hindi, and this mix of chilly spices from northwestern India's cooler climates brings a sense of heat both to the mouth and the soul.

Fenugreek: This herbal tree is found for its surprisingly bitter, somewhat sweet leaves, rich and round with a mild crunch.

Cinnamon's flavor and scent are distinctively woody, stinky, and velvety, and it has a warming effect on the palate.

Coconuts: Coconut milk and oils are essential in Northern Indian cooking, commonly used in curries.

Cumin has a distinct musty, earthy taste with some yellowish notes, making it an essential component in garam masala and chili powder.

Mint: This calming herb has a surprisingly fresh, herbal, sweet taste that goes well with lamb recipes and is used in raitas and curries.

Cardamom is a spice that is used in cooking. Cardamom has a lime, herbal, soapy taste with some bright yellow notes, making it an essential spice in garam masala.

Turmeric is a dried powdered root with a musky, oaky scent and a peppery, mildly bitter taste.

Chiles are native to South America and were brought to India by the Dutch.

Tamarind: Also known as Indian date, condensed tamarind paste is used to give curries and sauces a sour taste.

Cloves have a heavy, pungent, soft, almost spicy taste.

Cilantro: Cilantro (clean cilantro) has a waxy, citrusy, and soapy taste and fragrance.

Chapter 2: Indian Appetizers Recipes

2.1 Nippattu

Cooking Time: 30 minutes
Serving Size: 15-20
Ingredients:
- ¼ cup water or less
- Oil for frying
- ¾ teaspoon salt or as required
- 2 tablespoon hot oil
- 2 sprigs curry leaves
- 1 teaspoon red chili powder
- 1 cup rice flour
- 2 tablespoon dry coconut
- 1 tablespoon sesame seeds
- 2 tablespoon all-purpose flour
- ¼ cup peanuts
- 3 tablespoon fried gram
- 2 tablespoon chiroti rava

Method:
1. Dry roast groundnuts in a skillet until the skin begins to peel.
2. Add the dry coconut and bake for 20-30 seconds with the groundnut.
3. In a machine, combine all of the ingredients.
4. Set that aside after pulsing it into a gritty powder.
5. Add rice flour to the same pot and dry bake for two minutes on medium heat.
6. Insert the all-purpose starch and rava, and proceed to roast for 1 minute more.

7. Merge fine groundnut dust, dried chili powder, minced curry leaves, green onions, and salts in this roast rice flour.
8. Add the oil for frying over medium-high heat.
9. Pick the rolled pastry and gently place it in the hot oil.
10. Take the fried nippattu out of the oil and serve.

2.2 Thattai

Cooking Time: 40 minutes
Serving Size: 25 thattai
Ingredients:
For Roasting
- 1 cup rice flour
- 1 tablespoon urad dal

Other Ingredients
- 10 tablespoons water
- Oil as required
- ½ teaspoon red chili powder
- 2 tablespoons coconut
- ½ teaspoon salt
- 1 teaspoon white sesame seeds
- 1 tablespoon chana dal
- ¼ teaspoon asafoetida powder
- 1 tablespoon chana dal
- 1 tablespoon curry leaves
- 1 tablespoon butter

Method:
1. Wash the chana dal and keep it in hot water for a few minutes.
2. A hardpan should be heated. Toss in the urad dal.
3. For 2 minutes, gently roast the urad dal.
4. Add rice flour to the same plate.

5. Fry the corn starch on moderate to medium heat, often moving, until it is soft to the touch.
6. Keep the roasted urad dal and grind it in a small mixer.
7. Add roasted chana dal as well.
8. Combine the rest of the ingredients, as well as the spices.
9. Mix the butter and flour with your fingertips.
10. To make a semi-soft dough, combine all ingredients and knead until smooth.
11. In a skillet, keep oil for slow cooking.
12. Shape the dough into little balls.
13. Put softly in the hot oil.
14. Start frying the thattai on medium heat.
15. Fry the thattai until it is crisp and golden brown.

2.3 Shankarpali

Cooking Time: 1 hour
Serving Size: 1 jar
Ingredients:
- 3 to 3.5 tablespoon milk
- 2 tablespoon ghee
- ½ cup regular sugar
- 1 pinch salt
- ½ cup Rava
- 1.5 cups all-purpose flour

Method:
1. In a dry mixer, dust the sugar and set it aside.
2. To begin, salt the flour and sieve it.
3. The crushed sugar should then be sieved.
4. The oil should be warm.
5. Make a breadcrumb-like texture by mixing the fat into the flour mix.

6. Heat the milk in the microwave.
7. Then, one tablespoon at a time, insert the hot milk and whisk to a strong, tight mixture.
8. Cover and set aside for thirty minutes.
9. In a skillet, heat the oil for slow cooking.
10. Divide the dough into two parts is a good idea.
11. Transfer 8 of these cuts into the pan softly.
12. If you have a larger skillet, you can cook more.
13. Fry the shankarpali until golden brown.
14. Create diamond-shaped pieces out of the other slice of dough in the same way.
15. Fry such cuts too in quantities and serve.

2.4 Namak Para

Cooking Time: 1 hour 5 minutes
Serving Size: 4
Ingredients:
- Salt to taste
- Oil for frying
- 2 to 3 tablespoon oil
- ½ to ¾ cup water
- 1 teaspoon cumin seeds
- ¼ teaspoon baking soda
- 1 teaspoon carom seeds
- 1 teaspoon black pepper
- 1 cup all-purpose flour
- 1 cup wheat flour

Method:
1. Combine the whole wheat grain, wheat bread, white vinegar, and salt in a large mixing bowl.

2. Carom seeds can be included now.
3. Combine the carom seeds and the remaining sieved flours.
4. Start kneading the dough with the water.
5. Shape the dough into medium-sized spheres and roll them in flour.
6. Create criss-cross shapes on the rolling dough with a sharp blade.
7. Take the diamond-shaped designs from the skillet and pan-fry them in hot oil until lightly browned and crispy.
8. When they have cooled down, place them in an airtight container.
9. Namak para can be served with tea or as a snack.

2.5 Jhal Muri

Cooking Time: 15 minutes
Serving Size: 3
Ingredients:
Main Ingredients
- 1 teaspoon lemon juice
- 2 tablespoons coconut
- 1 teaspoon mustard oil
- 3 tablespoons coriander leaves
- 2 cups puffed rice
- ¼ cup roasted peanuts
- 3 tablespoons chana chur
- ¼ cup onions
- 1 to 2 green chilies
- ½ teaspoon ginger
- ¼ cup tomato
- ½ cup boiled potatoes
- ¼ cup cucumber
Spice Powders
- ½ teaspoon black salt

- ½ teaspoon rock salt
- ¼ teaspoon garam masala powder
- 1 teaspoon mango powder
- ½ teaspoon coriander powder
- ¼ teaspoon black pepper
- ½ teaspoon red chili powder
- ½ teaspoon cumin powder

Method:
1. To begin, finely chop the vegetables.
2. Set them aside for now.
3. Heat a wok over moderate to medium heat.
4. Put two cups of puffed rice into the mixture.
5. Turn off the heat and place the pan on the counter.
6. The fire from the skillet will roast and aromatize the spice powders.
7. Combine the puffed rice and seasoning powders in a mixing bowl.
8. Add ¼ cup roasted peanuts to the mix.
9. The coarsely diced onions, peppers, mushrooms, diced peppers, and ginger are then added.
10. After that, squirt one teaspoon of lime juice all over.
11. Re-blend gently.
12. Add sev to the mixture. You may also use chana chur rather than sev.
13. Coriander leaf should be added at this stage.
14. Taste and season with more salt, lime juice, or seasoning powders if desired.
15. Jhal muri should be served right away.

2.6 Spring Rolls

Cooking Time: 1 hour
Serving Size: 3
Ingredients:
Filling

- 1½ tablespoon oyster sauce
- 2 teaspoon soy sauce
- 1½ cups green cabbage
- 1 teaspoon cornflour
- 1½ cups carrot
- 1½ cups bean sprouts
- 1 tablespoon oil
- 400g pork
- 6 shiitake mushrooms
- 2 garlic cloves

Spring Rolls

- 1 tablespoon water
- Oil for frying
- 2 teaspoon cornflour
- 20 spring roll wrappers

Sweet and Sour Sauce

- 2 tablespoon tomato ketchup
- 2 teaspoon soy sauce
- ½ cup apple cider vinegar
- 1/3 cup brown sugar
- 2 tablespoon water
- 2 teaspoon cornflour

Method:
1. In a pan or wok, melt the oil over medium temperature.

2. Insert the garlic and whisk rapidly before adding the bacon.
3. Carrots, bean sprouts, lettuce, and mushrooms are all good additions.
4. Cook for three minutes until it has ripened veggies.
5. Cook for two minutes, or until the liquid has evaporated, adding cornflour, sesame oil, and oyster sauce as needed.
6. In a small bowl, combine cornstarch and water.
7. Fill a skillet or big saucepan halfway with oil to twice the height of the spring rolls.
8. Heat on high for a few minutes before hot.
9. Put spring rolls in the oils and fry, turning regularly, for two minutes, or until deep yellow. Repeat for the rest of the spring rolls.
10. Offer with Sweet and Tamarind Chutney while it is still hot!

2.7 Punugulu

Cooking Time: 30 minutes
Serving Size: 2-3
Ingredients:
- Salt as required
- Oil for deep frying
- 3 teaspoon coriander leaves
- 1 teaspoon cumin seeds
- ½ inch ginger
- 1 or 2 green chilies
- 1 cup idli batter
- 1 small onion
- 6 curry leaves
- 1 tablespoon rava

Method:

1. In a mixing dish, combine 1 cup idli mixture or dosa mixture.
2. Insert two to three teaspoon cilantro leaves, chopped garlic, Rava, cabbage, chopped cabbage, curry leaf, sliced mustard seeds, garlic, green chilies, two to three teaspoon cardamom leaves.
3. In a wok or skillet, heat the oil for slow cooking.
4. The exterior should be smooth, while the interior should be warm and plush.
5. If the mixture is too thick, a few teaspoons of water should be added.
6. In moderate oil, drop tablespoons of the batter.
7. Turn over until the sides are pale golden, and clear.
8. Fry them in medium-high heat, rotating them a few times to ensure even browning.
9. Punugulu is best served hot or warm with almond or nut chutney.

2.8 Vegetable Cutlets

Cooking Time: 45 minutes
Serving Size: 3

Ingredients:

- ⅓ cup bread crumbs
- 3 tablespoons oil
- 2 tablespoons all-purpose flour
- 3 tablespoons water
- ½ cup boiled carrots
- ½ teaspoon masala powder
- 3 tablespoons bread crumbs
- 1 cup boiled potatoes
- ¼ teaspoon red chili powder
- ½ teaspoon cumin powder
- ½ inch ginger

- ½ cup fresh green peas

Method:

1. In a broiler pan or heat cooker, thoroughly cook the potato, cabbage, and green peas.
2. When the vegetables are cooling, finely chop four to five slices of toast in a mixing bowl or blender to make bread crumbs.
3. Set aside the bread crumbs on a sheet or plate.
4. Slice and cut the carrots and potatoes.
5. Use a spoon or a masher to smash them.
6. Mix with the rest of the ingredients.
7. Add two tablespoon all-purpose starch and three tablespoon liquid in a separate small bowl.
8. Put the cutlet combination on a plate, then.
9. In a skillet, heat two to three tablespoons of oil for deep frying.
10. Then thinly roll the cutlet in breadcrumbs.
11. Remove any leftover bread crumbs before placing them in the medium-hot liquid.
12. Flip a few more times to ensure that all of the vegetables are cooked through.

Chapter 3: Indian Breakfast Recipes

3.1 Soft Idli

Cooking Time: 9 hours 25 minutes
Serving Size: 30 idli
Ingredients:
- 1 teaspoon rock salt
- Oil as required
- ¼ teaspoon fenugreek seeds
- Water
- ½ cup whole urad dal
- ¼ cup thick poha
- 1 cup regular rice

Method:
1. Both normal and preboiled rice should be picked and rinsed.
2. Fill the container halfway with water.
3. Individually soak the urad dal and methi seeds in liquid for five hours.
4. Drain the urad dal that has been soaked.
5. For a few seconds, grind the urad dal, methi seed, and ¼ cup of the allocated water.
6. Then pour in the remaining ¼ cup of water. Grind until the batter is thick and moist.
7. To form a delicious batter, ground the rice in quantities.
8. Grease the idli molds and set them aside.
9. In a slow cooker or hotplate, pour the mixture into the molds and steam the idli.
10. Heat for 15 to 20 minutes, or until the idlis are cooked through.

11.   Offer the hot steaming idli with sambar and mango chutney.

3.2 Crispy Dosa

Cooking Time: 14 hours
Serving Size: 15 dosa
Ingredients:
Dosa Batter
- 1 teaspoon rock salt
- Ghee or oil
- ½ teaspoon methi seeds
- 3 tablespoons flattened rice
- 1 tablespoon chana dal
- 1 tablespoon toor dal
- ¾ cup idli rice
- ½ cup urad dal gota
- ¾ cup Sona masoori rice

Potato Masala
- ½ teaspoon salt
- Cilantro to garnish
- 15 curry leaves
- ½ teaspoon turmeric powder
- 4 medium potatoes
- 1 medium onion
- 1-2 green chilies
- 6 cashews broken
- 1 teaspoon ginger
- 1 tablespoon oil
- ¼ teaspoon asafoetida
- 1 teaspoon chana dal
- ½ teaspoon mustard seeds

Method:

1. Transfer sona masoori grain, toor dal, urad dal gota, and methi seeds, in a big mixing cup.
2. Pour the water from the grain, dals, and poha before blending it in a high-powered blender.
3. Now, pass the mixture to the Instant Pot's steel pan.
4. One teaspoon rock salt can be added to the mixture.
5. Pour the salt into the mixture for two minutes with your hands.
6. In a medium-sized tub, heat one tablespoon of oil.
7. Toss in the chana dal, cashew nuts, and spice, minced.
8. Add the chopped onion, diced peppers, and coriander seeds after that.
9. Cook for about two minutes, or until the vegetables are softened.
10. Add the cinnamon and pepper to the boiling and whipped potatoes.
11. On medium-high fire, heat a cast iron pan.
12. Cut an onion in half, pierce it with a blade, and then drop it in oil.
13. Then begin preparing the dosa. Fill a ladle halfway with batter and dump it into the pan's middle.
14. Drizzle peanut oil or butter all over the dosa, as well as in the middle.
15. Fold in the cooked potato masala.
16. Prepare all of the dosas in the same manner.
17. Serve fried masala dosas immediately with sambar, coriander coconut lime pickle, or tomatillo salsa.

3.3 Uttapam

Cooking Time: 40 minutes
Serving Size: 8
Ingredients:
- 1 teaspoon kosher salt
- ¼ cup water
- 4 cups Idli Batter

Toppings
- ½ cup cilantro
- ¼ cup ghee
- 2 tomatoes
- 2 to 4 green chilies
- 1 medium red onion

Method:
1. To make a pancake-like texture, add salt and sugar to the idli batter.
2. To make a 6-inch croissant, spread around two spoons full of batter.
3. First, on the uttapam, place one tablespoon onions, pepper, ¼ teaspoon green chili, and ½ tablespoon coriander.
4. With a small silicone spoon, gently pick up the uttapam, coming in from the sides and touching the middle, and turn it over.
5. As the onions begin to caramelize, fry the strong part for 1 to 2 minutes.
6. Remove the uttapam and eat with mango pickle or cilantro leaf chutney and paratha, top side up.
7. Repeat for the rest of the batter.

3.4 Pesarattu

Cooking Time: 4 hours 20 minutes
Serving Size: 7
Ingredients:
For Batter
- 1 tablespoon rice flour
- Salt to taste
- 2 tablespoon chana dal
- Water as required
- 1 cup moong dal

Other Ingredients
- 1-inch ginger
- 1 green chili
- Half onion
- Seven teaspoon oil

Method:
1. First, soak chana dal and mong dal for at minimum up to eight hours in a big mixing cup.
2. Drain the water and mix the batter until it is creamy.
3. Place in a big mixing cup.
4. To put additional crispiness, add corn starch.
5. Season with salt to taste.
6. Shake the batter thoroughly until it reaches the strength of the dosa batter.
7. Using a spoon, spill a ladleful of batter onto a frying pan.
8. Place it thinly in a clockwise direction.
9. Over the pessarattu, spread a little coarsely diced onions, jeera, chili - pepper, and oil.
10. Strip the dosa from the ends gradually.
11. And then fold it into a triangle or some other shape you like.
12. Serve pessarattu with warm uppitu, allam sorbet, or mango pickle as a finishing touch.

3.5 Egg Toast

Cooking Time: 1 toast
Serving Size: 30 minutes

Ingredients:
- Salt, to taste
- Pepper, to taste
- 1 egg
- 3 tablespoons shredded cheese
- ½ tablespoon butter
- 1 slice bread

Method:
1. To make a bowl, press it down on the middle of the loaf with a spoon.
2. Spread the butter around the sides of the loaf and crack the egg into the jar.
3. Spread melted cheese along the bread's sides.
4. Season with salt and pepper and cook for fifteen minutes at 400°F.
5. A runny yolk will result after ten minutes, while a firmer yolk will result after fifteen minutes.

3.6 Egg Paratha

Cooking Time: 30 minutes
Serving Size: 2
Ingredients:
- 2 tablespoon coriander leaves
- ½ teaspoon garam masala
- ¼ cup onions
- 1 green chili
- 2 cups whole wheat flour
- 1 tablespoon oil
- 2 eggs
- A pinch of salt

Method:
1. Add flour, pepper, and oils to a measuring bowl, and whisk the combination into a flat dough with 1 cup of water.
2. If the flour seems to be dry, apply a little more liquid. Knead thoroughly.
3. Make four balls out of the dough.
4. Whisk together the eggs, carrots, chili, coriander, curry powder, and salt in a mixing cup. Set aside for now.
5. Put the rolled pastry on a frying pan and bake on both sides for 1-2 minutes.
6. Cook for another minute after adding a little oil to the surface.
7. Create a slit as soon as the edges begin to crisp.
8. More oil should be drizzled on the paratha, and the layer should be softly pressed with the back of the knife.

3.7 Egg Mayo Sandwich

Cooking Time: 35 minutes
Serving Size: 4
Ingredients:
- Salt and pepper to taste
- ¼ teaspoon paprika
- 1 teaspoon yellow mustard
- ¼ cup green onion
- ½ cup mayonnaise
- 8 eggs

Method:
1. In a frying pan, crack the egg and coat it with ice water.
2. Bring the water to a boil and then remove it from the heat.
3. Allow eggs to sit in hot water for 10 - 15 minutes, covered.
4. Take from the hot water, allow to cool before peeling and slicing.
5. In a mixing dish, combine the diced eggs, mayo, vinegar, and spring onions.
6. Season with parmesan, lime, and pepper.
7. Combine all ingredients in a mixing bowl and serve with your choice of bread or crackers.

Chapter 4: Indian Snack Recipes

4.1 Vegetable Pakora

Cooking Time: 20 minutes
Serving Size: 5
Ingredients:
Ketchup Chutney
- ½ teaspoon sugar
- ½ teaspoon salt
- 1 tablespoon water
- ½ tablespoon chaat masala
- ½ cup ketchup

Pakora Batter
- 1 cup luke-warm water
- Sunflower oil
- ½ cup cilantro leaves
- 1 yellow onion
- 2 cups besan
- ½ teaspoon baking powder
- 1 green chili pepper
- ¾ teaspoon sea salt
- 1 tablespoon red pepper flakes

Method:
1. In a mixing dish, combine all of the chutney components.
2. Half-fill an 8-inch cast-iron pan or other heavy-bottom pot with grease.
3. Preheat the oil to 375 degrees Fahrenheit.
4. Combine the besan, dried chili flakes, flour, icing sugar, sliced chili pepper, coriander, and diced onion in a big mixing cup.

5. Slowly drizzle in the water, constantly stirring with a spoon or your fingers.
6. When the oil is hot enough, gently drop a heaping tablespoon of mixture into it.
7. Fry the pakoras until they are a pecan-brown color.
8. Then use a cooling rack over a baking sheet, clean the pakoras.
9. Continue for the remaining hitter.
10. Serve the hot pakoras with the Tomato sauce Chutney straight away.

4.2 Onion Pakoras

Cooking Time: 30 minutes
Serving Size: 4
Ingredients:
- Water as required
- Salt as required
- 1 pinch baking soda
- Oil as required
- 1 teaspoon carom seeds
- 1 pinch asafoetida
- 2 medium onions
- ½ teaspoon garam masala powder
- ¼ teaspoon turmeric powder
- 1 cup gram flour
- 1 tablespoon coriander leaves
- 2 teaspoon green chilies

Method:
1. Finely chop the onions and place them in a blending dish.
2. Add the chopped green chilies as well.
3. Carom seeds, fenugreek seeds, asafoetida, and salt are added to the pan.

4. Combine all of the ingredients thoroughly.
5. Toss in the gram flour.
6. To make a moderate batter, add the appropriate volume of water.
7. With a fork or your hands, thoroughly combine the ingredients.
8. Transfer tablespoons of the flour to the hot oil.
9. Turn the pakoras over with a slotted spoon when they're almost done and begin to fry.
10. Fry them until they are crispy and fluffy.
11. Remove with a slotted spoon and wash on paper towels to extract any extra oil.
12. Slit green peppers are fried in the same oil.
13. Season the green chilies with salt and toss well.

4.3 Mysore Bonda

Cooking Time: 20 minutes
Serving Size: 4
Ingredients:

- 1 cup all-purpose flour
- ½ teaspoon cooking soda
- 1 cup yogurt
- ¼ cup rice flour
- 3 green chilies
- 1 tablespoon coconut pieces
- Salt - to taste
- 1 teaspoon cumin seeds
- 1 teaspoon ginger
- 1 cup water
- Oil - to fry

Method:
1. Combine the curd and the water in a mixing bowl. Let it aside for now.
2. In a mixing cup, combine all-purpose flour, rice flour, sugar, and soda; stir to combine, then apply buttermilk to create a vada batter texture.
3. Now add the cumin, thinly sliced coconut, diced peppers, coarsely diced ginger, and stir well. Set aside for 1 hour.
4. Heat the oil for frying, then cut the dough into small round bondas and place them in the oil to fry on low heat.
5. Once it has become a light golden hue, extract it. Serve with mango pickle on the side.

4.4 Churumuri

Cooking Time: 10 minutes
Serving Size: 2
Ingredients:
- 1 teaspoon lemon juice
- ¼ cup sev

- 1 green chili
- 3 tablespoons coriander leaves
- 2 cups puffed rice
- 1 small carrot
- 2 tablespoons green mango
- ¼ cup peanuts
- 1 small to medium onion
- 1 medium tomato
- 1 teaspoon red chili powder
- ¼ to ⅓ teaspoon salt
- 3 pinches black salt
- 1 tablespoon coconut oil
- 3 pinches turmeric powder

Method:
1. Vegetables should be peeled, rinsed, and finely chopped.
2. In a bowl or skillet, heat ½ tablespoon essential oils.
3. Place the puffed rice on top.
4. Puffed rice grain should be roasted until crisp and chewy.
5. Put the puffed rice in the skillet and wait two to four minutes.
6. Combine the rest of the ingredients and stir well.
7. Dress with a pinch of black salt and a pinch of common salt or salt to taste.
8. Cover the puffed rice finely with cocoa butter, peanuts, seasoning powders, and salt.
9. Add the coarsely diced vegetables, green chilies, and coriander leaves at this stage.
10. Apply the lemon juice right now.
11. Mix all in fast and serve the churumuri right away.

4.5 Crispy Corn

Cooking Time: 15 minutes
Serving Size: 3
Ingredients:
For Boiling
- 2 cup sweet corn
- 1 teaspoon salt
- 4 cup water

For Frying
- ¼ teaspoon salt
- Oil
- 1 tablespoon all-purpose flour
- ¼ teaspoon pepper powder
- ¼ cup rice flour
- ¼ cup cornflour

For Masala
- 2 tablespoon capsicum
- 2 tablespoon coriander
- ¼ teaspoon salt
- 2 tablespoon onion
- ¼ teaspoon cumin powder
- ½ teaspoon amchur
- ½ teaspoon red chili powder

Method:
1. First, bring 4 cups of water and one teaspoon of salt to a boil in a large pot.
2. Boil for a moment after adding 2 cups of sweet corn.
3. To extract excess water, extract the sweet corn.
4. ¼ cup cornflour, ¼ cup corn grits, one tablespoon all-purpose flour, ¼ teaspoon spice powder, and ¼ teaspoon salt are now added to the mixture.
5. Mix thoroughly to ensure that the flour is evenly distributed in the green beans.

6. Deep fry in hot oil while maintaining a medium fire.
7. Cook on medium heat, stirring regularly until lightly browned.
8. ½ teaspoon chili flakes, ¼ teaspoon smoked paprika, ½ teaspoon amchur, and ¼ teaspoon salt are added to the mixture.
9. Mix thoroughly to ensure that all of the spices are evenly distributed.
10. 2 tablespoon cabbage, two tablespoon purple cabbage, and two tablespoon coriander are indeed good additions.

4.6 Chakli

Cooking Time: 1 hour 10 minutes
Serving Size: 12
Ingredients:
- ½ cup water
- Oil for frying
- ¼ teaspoon turmeric
- 2 teaspoons kosher salt
- 1.5 teaspoons ajwain
- 1 tablespoon red chili powder
- 2 cups Bhajani flour
- ¼ cup water hot
- Two tablespoons sesame seeds
- ¼ cup oil

Method:
1. In a mixing pot, add the flour.
2. Add ¼ cup warm oil and ¼ cup warm water to the pan.
3. Combine the red chili powder, crow hop seeds, fenugreek, salt, and sesame seeds in a bowl. With a spoon, combine everything.

4. To make a soft pastry, gradually apply ice water and whisk the flour.
5. In a deep fryer or skillet, heat the oil over low heat.
6. In the chakli press, place the chakli disk with the circular pattern in the center.
7. Cautiously drop chakli into the hot liquid one at a time, being cautious not to overcrowd the deep fryer.
8. Turn them off one after three minutes and fry on the middle to low heat before light brown.
9. Before introducing the next amount of chakli, note to turn up the oil's heat too high.

4.7 Dahi Vada

Cooking Time: 40 minutes
Serving Size: 10

Ingredients:
- ½ teaspoon salt
- Oil for frying
- 1-inch ginger
- ¾ cup split black gram lentils
- 1 green chili pepper
- 3 tablespoon yellow lentils

Assembling Ingredients
- ¼ teaspoon red chili powder
- Cilantro leaves chopped
- 2 tablespoon cilantro chutney
- ½ teaspoon ground cumin
- ½ teaspoon sugar adjust
- ¼ cup tamarind chutney
- ¼ teaspoon salt adjust
- 2 cups yogurt chilled

Method:
1. Clean the lentils several times in a wide bowl before the water runs clear.
2. Pour the water that has been soaking in the pan.
3. In a mixer, combine the ginger, green chili pepper, cinnamon, and lentils.
4. Crush on medium to a low level until the batter is nearly flat.
5. To keep the lentil batter soft and moist, rapidly whip it.
6. In a skillet, heat the oil. Before creating the Vada's, please ensure the oil is hot.
7. Then use a spoon or an ice cream plunger, drop the batter into the oil.
8. When you lower the Vada's in the oil, use a spoon to avoid pouring oil over it.
9. Drench the vadas for about fifteen minutes in a lukewarm bath.
10. To extract extra moisture, take each vada and press down it between your palms.
11. Season the yogurt with sugar and salt and mix it.
12. In a pan, position the softened vadas.
13. The yogurt should be poured over them.
14. Spray the ground cumin powder and red chili powder over the tamarind and mint coriander chutneys.
15. Serve with a sprinkling of cilantro on top.

4.8 Dahi Kebab

Cooking Time: 12 hours 25 minutes
Serving Size: 6
Ingredients:
- 2 tablespoon cornflour
- Oil for deep frying
- ½ teaspoon pepper

- ¼ cup bread crumbs
- 2 tablespoon dry fruits
- Salt to taste
- 2 cups curd
- 1 green chili
- 2 tablespoon coriander leaves
- 1 cup paneer
- 1-inch ginger
- ½ small onion

Method:
1. To begin, make a smooth and creamy custard.
2. One cup of crushed paneer is also added.
3. Add the onion, spice, chili, coriander, and dried fruits to the mix as well.
4. Insert salt and cracked pepper to taste.
5. Make sure the paneer and hanging curd are thoroughly mixed.
6. To extract excess moisture, dust the tortillas with cornflour.
7. In a hot pan, deep-fry the patties.
8. Cook, stirring regularly, on medium heat.
9. Fry the patties or kababs until they are nicely browned.
10. Eventually, serve Dahi ke kabab with risotto or sauce made from pudina.

Chapter 5: Indian Lunch Recipes

5.1 Cauliflower Korma

Cooking Time: 1 hour 10 minutes
Serving Size: 6
Ingredients:
For the Roasted Cauliflower

- ½ teaspoon cumin
- 2 teaspoon salt
- ½ teaspoon turmeric
- ½ teaspoon coriander
- 1 tablespoon garam masala
- ½ teaspoon cinnamon
- 3 tablespoon oil
- 1½ kg cauliflower florets

For the Korma Curry

- 2 teaspoon sugar
- Salt and pepper to taste
- 2 cups stock
- 1 cup cream
- 1½ cups raw cashew nuts
- ½ teaspoon cinnamon
- 1 teaspoon chili powder
- 1 teaspoon turmeric
- ½ teaspoon cardamom
- 2 tablespoon butter
- 1 teaspoon coriander
- 1 teaspoon cumin
- 1 large onion
- 3 teaspoon crushed ginger
- 1 tablespoon garam masala
- 4 garlic cloves

Method:

1. Preheat the oven to 400 degrees Fahrenheit.
2. Mix all of the food items for the roasted cauliflower.
3. Put the cauliflower in the oven and bake for thirty minutes or until it is caramelized and crispy.
4. Meanwhile, soak the walnuts for ten minutes in hot water.
5. In the butter, cook the onion, parsley, and ginger until sticky and citrusy.
6. Cook for another minute after adding the spices.
7. Wash the cashews and blend them with the flour mixture, stock, and yogurt in a food processor.
8. Mix thoroughly, then sprinkle with salt, pepper, and sucrose in a frying pan.
9. Enable for ten minutes of gentle simmering after adding the roasted cauliflower.
10. Season with salt and pepper and serve with rice, hummus, and buttered cashews.

5.2 Chicken Madras Curry

Cooking Time: 35 minutes
Serving Size: 3-4
Ingredients:
- 400g can tomatoes
- Small pack coriander
- 1-2 teaspoon chili powder
- 4 chicken breasts
- 1 onion
- 1 teaspoon cumin
- 1 teaspoon coriander
- 2 garlic cloves
- 1 tablespoon vegetable oil
- ½ teaspoon turmeric

- ½ red chili
- 1 ginger

Method:
1. In a mixing bowl, blitz the garlic, cherry tomatoes, lime, and chili flakes until coarse paste forms.
2. In a medium skillet, warm the veggie oil, add the paste, and cook over medium heat until it is loosened.
3. Stir in the turmeric, cumin seeds, coriander seeds, and hot chili flakes, then cook for a few minutes before adding the four chicken thighs.
4. Mix everything to make sure it is all covered in the spice mixture.
5. Cook until the chicken is pale in color.
6. Pan and simmer on low heat for thirty minutes, till the chicken is soft, adding 400g diced tomatoes and a large pinch of salt.
7. Serve with rice after stirring in a tiny bag of coriander.

5.3 Ennai Kathirikai Kulambu

Cooking Time: 40 minutes
Serving Size: 4
Ingredients:
Other Ingredients
- Salt as required
- 1 teaspoon jaggery powder
- ¼ teaspoon turmeric powder
- 1 cup water
- 10 curry leaves
- 2 pinch asafoetida
- 3 tablespoons sesame oil
- ½ teaspoon mustard seeds
- 250 grams small brinjals

For Spice Paste
- ¼ teaspoon black pepper
- ⅓ cup water
- 2 teaspoons poppy seeds
- ½ teaspoon cumin seeds
- 2 dry red chilies
- 5 tablespoons fresh coconut
- 1 teaspoon urad dal
- ¼ teaspoon fenugreek seeds
- 2 teaspoons gingelly oil
- 2 teaspoons chana dal
- 1 tablespoon coriander seeds

For Tamarind Pulp
- ½ cup hot water
- 1 tablespoon tamarind

Method:

1. Heat 2 tablespoons gingelly oil in a shallow saucepan or wok and transfer 2 tablespoons chana dal.
2. Fry chana dal until light perfect, stirring frequently.
3. After that, add one teaspoon of urad dal.
4. After that, season with salt and pepper.
5. Insert two teaspoons pumpkin seeds and 14 teaspoon fenugreek
6. Add five spoonfuls of grated coconut after that.
7. Turn off the heat and place the pan on the counter.
8. To make a smooth paste, combine all of the ingredients in a blender.
9. After this, cut every brinjal in half.
10. In a skillet, heat three tablespoons of gingelly oil. 12 teaspoon tomato sauce should be added.
11. Then insert 7 to 9 curry leaves and two pinches of asafoetida into the pan.
12. Combine the brinjal and seasonings in a mixing bowl.
13. Combine the ingredients that have been prepared.
14. Serve after a final mix.

5.4 Chana Dal

Cooking Time: 1 hour
Serving Size: 4

Ingredients:

- 1 teaspoon red chile flakes
- 3 tablespoons cilantro
- 6 whole cloves
- 4 large garlic cloves
- 1 cup split chickpeas

- 1 ½ teaspoons turmeric
- 1 bay leaf
- 1 teaspoon salt
- 2 tablespoons sunflower oil
- ½ teaspoon cardamom

Method:
1. In a medium skillet, give the chana dal, fenugreek, cinnamon, lemon zest, salt, and 4 cups liquid to a boil.
2. Cook for another 20 minutes, adding 1 cup of water as needed.
3. Remove the bay leaf from the dish.
4. In a shallow dish, add the oil to start making the tadka.
5. Add the chilies to the hot oil and let them swirl for about thirty seconds until its aromatic.
6. Cook, keep stirring, till the garlic is moderate brown.
7. Spill the tadka into the dal and bring to a simmer softly.
8. Serve with coriander as a garnish.

5.5 Mughlai Biryani

Cooking Time: 1 hour 10 minutes
Serving Size: 4

Ingredients:
For Mughlai Biryani Gravy

- ½ teaspoon garam masala powder
- Salt as required
- ½ cup curd
- ⅔ cup water
- 4 tablespoon ghee
- 1 tablespoon ginger-garlic paste
- 2.5 to 3 cups veggies
- ⅓ cup green peas
- 9 black pepper
- 1 teaspoon caraway seeds
- ½ teaspoon red chili powder
- 3 green cardamoms
- 1 black cardamom
- 1-inch cinnamon
- 2 single strands of mace
- 12 almonds
- 1 tej patta
- 3 cloves
- 16 raisins
- 1 large onion
- 12 cashews

For Cooking Rice

- 5 cups water
- ½ teaspoon salt
- 3 cloves
- 3 green cardamoms
- 1.5 cups basmati rice

- 1 medium tej patta
- 2 to 3 mace
- 1-inch cinnamon

For Layering
- 2 tablespoon mint leaves
- 2 teaspoon rose water
- 3 tablespoon warm milk
- 200 grams Paneer

For White Paste
- 1 tablespoon melon seeds
- 10 to 12 almonds
- 2 tablespoon water
- 1 tablespoon coconut

Method:
1. After thirty minutes of soaking, drain the rice and set it aside.
2. 10 to 12 almonds and one tablespoon melon seeds should be soaked.
3. In a tiny grinder jar, combine them with one tablespoon of flaked coconut.
4. All of the vegetables should be rinsed, peeled, and chopped.
5. Take a pan with a thick bottom.
6. Take five cups of water and bring to a boil over high heat.
7. Now toss in the rice.
8. Cook the rice on a high heat setting.
9. Heat three to four tablespoons ghee in a slow cooker.
10. Fry the almonds, pecans, and cashew nuts.
11. Cook until the onions are golden brown and caramelized.
12. Place the cooker on the stovetop once more. Mix in the whole spice.
13. Toss in the mixed vegetables.
14. Insert the white paste that has been ground.

15.   Slow cook the veggie gravy for eight to nine minutes, stirring well.
16.   Spill half of the veggie gravy on top of the first layer.
17.   Add some paneer squares to the mix.
18.   Repeat layering with the residual veggie gravy.

5.6 Veg Pulao

Cooking Time: 50 minutes
Serving Size: 2
Ingredients:
For Pulao Masala Paste
- 1 teaspoon fennel
- ¼ cup water
- 1-inch cinnamon
- 5 cloves
- ½ cup coriander
- 2 chili
- 2 pod cardamom
- ¼ cup mint
- 2 clove garlic
- 1-inch ginger

For Veg Pulao
- 1 teaspoon salt
- 2 cup water
- ½ carrot
- ½ potato
- 2 tablespoon ghee
- ½ capsicum
- 2 tablespoon peas
- 1 tomato
- 5 beans
- 1 teaspoon cumin

- 1 bay leaf
- ½ teaspoon pepper
- 1-inch cinnamon
- 2 pod cardamom
- 3 cloves
- 5 cashew
- ½ onion
- 1 cup basmati rice

Method:
1. To begin, place whole cloves in a small blender.
2. Two tablespoon ghee, heated in a big wok, cumin, lemon zest, cloves, coriander, garlic, pepper, and cashews, are added to the pot.
3. Sauté on low heat until the spices become fragrant.
4. Put one tomato and continue to sauté.
5. Include vegetables as well.
6. Cook for a minute, just until the veggies are fragrant.
7. Please ensure the basmati rice is soaked for 20 minutes before adding the veggies.
8. The veg pulao is ready to eat after 20 minutes.

5.7 Brinjal Rice

Cooking Time: 30 minutes
Serving Size: 4
Ingredients:
- 1.5 cups basmati rice
For Ground Masala Paste
- ½ teaspoon fennel seeds
- 4 to 5 tablespoons water
- 2 cloves
- 2 green cardamoms
- 1 tablespoon coconut

- 1-inch cinnamon
- 3 tablespoons coriander leaves
- 2-inch ginger
- 7 medium garlic cloves
- 2 to 3 green chilies
- 3 tablespoons mint leaves

Other Ingredients
- ½ cup water
- Salt as required
- ¼ cup French beans
- 2 cups coconut milk
- ⅓ cup capsicum
- ⅓ cup green peas
- 3 tablespoons oil
- ⅓ cup tomatoes
- ½ to ¾ cup cauliflower florets
- 1 large tej patta
- ½ cup onions
- ½ cup carrots
- 2 cloves
- 1 green cardamom
- 1-inch cinnamon
- ½ cup potato

Method:
1. Soak 1.5 cups basmati rice in water for a few minutes.
2. Put spices in a tiny mixer jar and grind them.
3. In a 3 gallon slow cooker, heat three tablespoons of oil.
4. One-inch cloves, two garlic, and one green cinnamon can be added right away.
5. Fry spices for a few seconds before fragrant.
6. Then add a third of a cup of sliced tomatoes.
7. Now add the masala paste that has been ground.

8. After that, toss in the vegetables.
9. After that, add the rice.
10.   Cook for ten minutes on medium heat in a pressure cooker.
11.   With some raita, eat veg brinji grain.

5.8 Drumstick Sambar

Cooking Time: 35 minutes
Serving Size: 4
Ingredients:
For Sambar Powder
- Few curry leaves
- Pinch Hing
- 1 teaspoon chana dal
- 20 dried red chili
- 1 teaspoon coconut oil
- 1 tablespoon cumin
- ½ teaspoon methi
- ¼ cup coriander seeds
- 1 teaspoon urad dal

For Sambar
- ½ cup tamarind extract
- 2 tablespoon coriander
- 2 cup water
- 2 cup toor dal
- 3 teaspoon oil
- 1 teaspoon salt
- 20 pieces drumstick
- 1 teaspoon mustard
- 1 tomato
- ½ teaspoon turmeric
- 3 dried red chili
- Few curry leaves

- 7 shallots
- Pinch Hing

Method:
1. To begin, warm three teaspoon oil in a broad wok and splutter the tempering.
2. Sauté for two minutes with seven shallots.
3. As well, put one tomato in the pan and cook until it softens.
4. 12 teaspoon garlic, two tablespoons payasam powder, and one teaspoon salt are also added.
5. Cook for 20 minutes after adding the drumsticks.
6. Two cup toor dal and 1 cup water are now included.
7. Cover and cook over medium heat or until the flavors are completely absorbed.
8. 12 cup tamarind extract should also be added and thoroughly mixed.
9. Boil for another five minutes.
10. Finally, toss in 2 tablespoons coriander and serve with hot steamed rice.

5.9 Navratan Korma

Cooking Time: 50 minutes
Serving Size: 5
Ingredients:
- Pinch garam masala
- 2 tablespoons pineapple pieces

- 1 tablespoon pomegranate arils
- Pinch cardamom powder
- 2 onion
- 5-6 whole cashews
- Pinch saffron
- 1-inch ginger
- 4 large garlic cloves
- 1 green chili
- 20 cashews
- ¼ cup cream
- 2 teaspoons golden raisins
- 1 tablespoon poppy seeds
- One teaspoon salt or to taste
- ¾ teaspoon sugar
- 3 cups water
- ¼ teaspoon red chili powder
- ¾ cup water
- 1 teaspoon coriander powder
- ½ teaspoon cumin powder
- 1 tablespoon ghee
- 1 bay leaf
- 1 medium potato
- 1/3 cup green peas
- 1 tablespoon oil
- 2 cloves
- 1 large carrot
- 14 green beans
- 1 cup cauliflower florets
- 3 whole green cardamom

Method:
1. Insert 3 cups water, cabbage, carrot, cloves, green chili, cashews, and pumpkin seeds in a big pan.
2. Cook for 10 minutes on medium-high heat.

3. Chop all of the vegetables, keeping in mind to chop them thinly.
4. In the meantime, add cabbage, shallots, onion, beans, and beans to a boiling water pan.
5. Cook for ten minutes over medium heat.
6. One tablespoon oil, heated in a wok.
7. Add the bay leaf, garlic, and cardamom to the pot.
8. Enable the spices to cook for a few minutes.
9. Insert the rosemary powder, cilantro, and red chili powder after the mixture has cooked for five minutes.
10. Add the vegetables and stir to combine.
11. Then stir in the milk.
12. Blend in the pomegranate, roasted cashew nuts, and pecans.
13. Insert the saffron milk that has been prepared as well.

Chapter 6: Indian Dinner Recipes

6.1 Mushroom Biryani

Cooking Time: 40 minutes
Serving Size: 3
Ingredients:
- 1 cup water
- ½ teaspoon rose water
- ½ teaspoon paprika
- ¾ teaspoon salt
- ¼ cup mint
- ½ teaspoon garam masala
- 1 cup basmati rice
- ½ cup coconut milk
- ¼ cup cilantro
- 2 tablespoons oil
- 2 teaspoons ginger-garlic paste
- 10 oz. white mushrooms
- 1 bay leaf
- 1 green chili
- 15 whole cashews
- 1 teaspoon shahi jeera
- 1 medium red onion
- 3 whole cloves
- 6 black peppercorns
- 1-inch cinnamon stick
- 4 whole green cardamom

Method:
1. Wash the basmati rice till the water is clear when you begin.

2. Transfer the seasoning to the Instant Pot's sauté feature.
3. And insert the green chili, tomato, and cashew nuts.
4. Cook for 3 minutes before adding the ginger-garlic paste and continuing to cook for two minutes.
5. Heat for 2 minutes after adding the mushrooms.
6. After that, whisk in the coconut milk.
7. Add the coriander and mint, diced.
8. The garam masala, cayenne pepper, and salt are then added.
9. Add the rice, which has been rinsed and washed.
10. Open the lid on the pot.
11. Cook for five minutes on elevated heat using the manual setting.
12. With a spoon, fluff the rice after opening the lid.
13. Serve mushrooms Biryani with yogurt or raita on the side.

6.2 Bisi Bele Bath

Cooking Time: 40 minutes
Serving Size: 3
Ingredients:
Other Ingredients
- 1 cup water
- 1 tablespoon ghee
- 1 cup toor dal
- 2½ cup rice
- ½ carrot
- ½ teaspoon jaggery
- ½ onions
- 5 beans
- 1½ teaspoon salt
- ¾ cup tamarind extract

- 2 cups water
- ¼ teaspoon turmeric
- ½ potato
- 2 tablespoon peanuts
- 2 tablespoon green peas

Bisi Bele Bath Masala

- 4 teaspoon coriander seeds
- Few curry leaves
- Pinch of hing
- 1 teaspoon oil
- 12 dried red chili
- 2 teaspoon poppy seeds
- 1 teaspoon sesame seeds
- 4 teaspoon chana dal
- 4 cloves
- 2 tablespoon dry coconut
- 3 pods cardamom
- 1-inch cinnamon
- 2 teaspoon urad dal
- ¼ teaspoon methi
- ½ teaspoon pepper
- 1 teaspoon jeera

For Tempering

- Few curry leaves
- 10 whole cashew
- 1 dried red chili
- Pinch of hing
- 1 teaspoon mustard
- 2 tablespoon ghee

Method:
1. Cook the vegetables, nuts, liquid, turmeric, and salts first.
2. Add the tamarind paste, jaggery, and vegetables at this stage.
3. Cook for ten minutes at a low temperature.

4. Fried toor dal, cooked rice, and 1 cup water are added next.
5. Boil for 20 minutes with bisi Bisi bele bath curry powder.
6. Offer bisi bele bath with boondi or a combination after adding the tempering.

6.3 Paneer Butter Masala

Cooking Time: 35 minutes
Serving Size: 4
Ingredients:
Other Ingredients
- ½ teaspoon Kasuri methi
- ¼ teaspoon garam masala
- 20 cubes paneer
- 2 tablespoon coriander
- 1 teaspoon salt
- 2 tablespoon cream
- 1 cup water
- ½ teaspoon sugar
- 2 tablespoon butter
- ¼ teaspoon garam masala
- ¼ teaspoon cumin powder
- 2 pods cardamom
- ¼ teaspoon turmeric
- 1 teaspoon red chili powder
- 1 bay leaf

For Onion Tomato Paste
- 2 tomato
- 10 cashew
- 1-inch ginger
- 3 clove garlic
- 1 teaspoon oil
- 1 onion

- 1 teaspoon butter

Method:
1. To begin, melt one teaspoon oil and one teaspoon oil in a broad wok.
2. Cook until the onion, carrot, and garlic have shrunk somewhat.
3. After a minute, apply the tomato and cashews.
4. Allow cooling entirely before transferring to the blender.
5. Blend until the paste is smooth.
6. Sauté 2 cardamom seeds and 1 star anise in oil in a wok.
7. Season with herbs and seasonings.
8. Sauté until the cloves are fragrant but not burned.
9. Mix in 2 tablespoons of milk as well.
10. Now softly fold in 20 pieces of paneer.
11. Last but not least, serve paneer butter chutney with roti or hummus.

6.4 Vangi Bath

Cooking Time: 25 minutes
Serving Size: 3
Ingredients:
For Rice
- 3 cup cooked rice
- 2 tablespoon coriander
- 1 teaspoon salt
- ½ teaspoon jaggery
- ¼ teaspoon turmeric
- ½ cup tamarind extract
- 2 tablespoon oil
- 1 dried red chili
- 2 brinjal

- 2 tablespoon peanut
- Few curry leaves
- 1 teaspoon mustard
- 1 teaspoon urad dal
- 1 teaspoon chana dal
- 1 teaspoon cumin

For Vangi Bath Masala Powder
- ½ cup dry coconut
- 20 dried red chili
- 1 tablespoon cumin
- 1 teaspoon methi
- 5-inch cinnamon
- ¼ cup urad dal
- ¼ cup chana dal
- 1 teaspoon clove
- 2 teaspoon oil
- ¼ cup coriander seeds
- 5 pods cardamom
- 2 teaspoon poppy seeds
- 1 mace

Method:

1. To begin, dry roast spice, cardamom, coriander, and mace in a big skillet.
2. Dry roast pumpkin seeds in the same pan until they begin to pop up.
3. Add one teaspoon of milk, chana dal, coriander seeds, urad dal, smoked paprika, and methi in a jar.
4. In a mixer, combine the roasted ingredients.
5. Without incorporating any liquid, blend to a powder form.
6. First, heat the oil in a big wok and add the cumin, chana dal, mustard, urad dal, and peanuts.
7. On medium heat, sauté and splutter.
8. Insert a few bay leaves and one red chili pepper at this stage.

9. Put two brinjals and cook for another two minutes.
10. Finally, toss in 2 tablespoons coriander and serve with raita.

6.5 Kashmiri Pulao

Cooking Time: 35 minutes
Serving Size: 4
Ingredients:
- ½ cup dried fruits
- 2-3 edible rose petals
- Salt to taste
- 2 tablespoon ghee
- ½ cup fresh cream
- 1 teaspoon sugar
- 2 cups basmati rice
- 1 bay leaf
- 2 cups milk
- ½ teaspoon cumin seeds
- 1 stick cinnamon
- 3 cardamom
- 3 cloves

Method:
1. Combine the milk, cream, salt, and spice in a mixing bowl.
2. Drain the rice and set it aside.
3. In a heavy skillet, melt the ghee and add the cumin seeds, cloves, black pepper, cardamom seeds, and spices.
4. When they begin to splutter, add the rice and continue cooking in the ghee.
5. Insert 12 cup water and the milk mixture
6. Bring to the boil, then reduce to low heat and cook until the chicken is finished.

7. Gently fold in the dried berries.
8. Serve warm, with rose petals on top.

6.6 Porsha Kuzhambu

Cooking Time: 45 minutes
Serving Size: 6
Ingredients:
For Coconut Paste
- ½ teaspoon cumin seeds
- 1 teaspoon raw rice
- ¼ teaspoon peppercorns
- ½ cup grated coconut
- 4 red chili
- ½ teaspoon cooking oil

Other Ingredients
- ¼ teaspoon turmeric powder
- 2 teaspoon salt
- ½ cup toor dal

Vegetables
- 1 carrot
- 1 drumstick
- 50 grams cucumber
- 50 grams elephant yam
- 2 brinjal
- 50 grams snake gourd

For Tempering
- 1 sprig of curry leaves
- ¼ teaspoon asafoetida
- 1 teaspoon mustard seeds
- 1 teaspoon split urad dal
- 1 teaspoon cooking oil

Method:

1. In a slow cooker, heat the thurdal until tender, then mash the dhal.
2. Soak the uncooked rice for a while in the water.
3. All of the veggies should be chopped into small sections.
4. Wash the raw rice in water for a few minutes.
5. Load the oil into a different pan and cook the red chilies and black peppercorns for a moment.
6. In a blender, combine the fried chilies, pepper, coconut, chopped garlic, and washed raw rice.
7. Use water, process the components into a smooth paste.
8. Finally, insert the ground mixture and get the kuzhambu to a simmer.
9. Load the oil into a different pan and add the bay leaves.
10. Now you can eat the Poritha Kuzhambu with boiled rice.

6.7 Potato Kurma

Cooking Time: 45 minutes
Serving Size: 5
Ingredients:
- 1 tablespoon sunflower oil
- Salt, as required
- 1 teaspoon coriander
- ½ teaspoon garam masala
- 3 potato
- ½ teaspoon turmeric powder
- 1- ½ teaspoon red chili
- 1 onion
- 1-inch cinnamon stick
- 1 teaspoon ginger garlic paste
- 1 bay leaf
- 2 tomatoes

Ingredients to Grind
- ½ cup fresh coconut
- 1 teaspoon cumin seeds
- 1 teaspoon fennel seeds

Method:
1. Cook the potatoes in the pressure cooker.
2. In a blender, combine all of the ingredients listed under "To Grinding" and crush them into a thick powder.
3. In a medium deep fryer, heat the oil.
4. Cinnamon, garlic, bay leaf, and coarsely diced onion are added to the pot.
5. Sauté for several minutes with the ginger garlic paste.
6. Heat until the vegetables have broken down into a sauce.
7. Heat until the cayenne pepper, dried chili powder, balsamic vinegar, and curry paste powder are mixed with the onion-tomato mixture.
8. Transfer the thinly sliced potatoes to the bowl and mix them well with the spicy combination. Serve immediately.

6.8 Matar Paneer

Cooking Time: 10 minutes
Serving Size: 2
Ingredients:
- Small pack coriander
- Naan bread, roti, or rice
- 150g frozen peas

- 1 teaspoon garam masala
- 1 tablespoon sunflower oil
- 1 green chili
- 4 large ripe tomatoes
- 225g paneer
- 1 teaspoon turmeric
- 1 teaspoon ground coriander
- 1 teaspoon ground cumin
- 2.5cm piece ginger

Method:

1. In a deep fryer, flame the oil over medium temperature until it shimmers.
2. Reduce the heat to low and add the paneer.
3. In a sauce, combine the ginger, smoked paprika, turmeric, coriander seeds, chili, and continue cooking.
4. Then use the back of a spoon, mix the tomato in.
5. Stirring occasionally for another two minutes after adding the peas, now stir in the paneer and season with garam masala.
6. Offer with peanut sauce, roti, or rice, divided into two bowls and topped with coriander leaves.

Chapter 7: Indian Desserts Recipes

7.1 Besan Lado Recipe

Cooking Time: 35 minutes
Serving Size: 10 lado
Ingredients:
- ¼ teaspoon cardamom powder
- 2 teaspoons nuts
- ½ cup powdered sugar
- ¼ cup ghee
- 1 cup gram flour

Method:
1. Transfer the ghee to a heavy-bottomed pan and melt it over low pressure.
2. Transfer the poured besan to the pan until the ghee has melted.
3. On medium heat, continue cooking constantly.
4. Switch off the heat in the bowl.
5. Then stir in the cardamom powder.
6. Combine the sugar and peanuts in a mixing bowl.
7. Integrate all of the ingredients in a large mixing bowl before the sugar and nuts are thoroughly mixed.
8. Pinch a little bowl out of the dough now.
9. To make a circular shape, press and roll across your palms.

7.2 Ras Malai Recipe

Cooking Time: 4 hours
Serving Size: 8
Ingredients:
For Rabri
- 5 almonds
- 10 cashews
- 2 tablespoon saffron milk
- 7 pistachios
- 1-liter milk
- ½ teaspoon cardamom powder
- ¼ cup sugar

For Chenna
- 2 tablespoon lemon juice
- 1 cup water
- 1-liter milk

For Sugar Syrup
- 8 cups water
- 1½ cup sugar

Method:
1. To begin, heat the milk.
2. In particular, stir in the lemon juice.
3. Drain and pinch the curdled milk to remove any extra water.
4. Start kneading after thirty minutes.
5. Also, make little balls and flatten them.
6. To begin, combine water and sugar.
7. Get the syrup to a boil for ten minutes.
8. Afterward, release the paneer balls that have been packed.
9. Cook for fifteen minutes with the lid on.
10. Get the milk to a boil.
11. Glucose, coriander powder, and saffron milk are also added.
12. Put it in the fridge for another 2-3 hours.

13. Place the chilled rabri over the balls now.
14. Finally, add a few nuts as a finishing touch.

7.3 Kaju Katli Recipe

Cooking Time: 25 minutes
Serving Size: 20 piece
Ingredients:
- 1 teaspoon ghee
- Edible silver leaves
- ¼ cup water
- ½ teaspoon rose water
- ½ cup white sugar
- 1 cup cashews

Method:
1. In a seasoning grinder, ground the cashews.
2. To make a smooth powder, combine all ingredients in a blender and blend until smooth.
3. In a medium-sized saucepan, combine the sugar and water.
4. Allow the sugar to dissolve and the mixture to boil for 1 minute.
5. On low pressure, keep swirling the combination.
6. Stir in one teaspoon of ghee.
7. Stir constantly; the dough will quit the pan's edges after about ten minutes on medium heat.
8. Move the flour to a piece of parchment paper until it is done.
9. So, with your fingertips, knead the dough until it is soft.
10. By slicing the dough horizontally and then vertically, you will make a diamond shape.
11. Remove the Kaju katli and serve.

7.4 Boondi Lado Recipe

Cooking Time: 40 minutes
Serving Size: 12
Ingredients:
For Boondi

- ¼ teaspoon baking soda
- Oil for deep frying
- 3 drops yellow color
- ¼ cup
- 1 cup gram flour

Other Ingredients

- 5 cloves
- ¼ teaspoon cardamom powder
- 2 tablespoon kishmish
- 2 tablespoon cashew
- 1 tablespoon butter

For Sugar Syrup

- ½ cup water
- 1¼ cup sugar

Method:
1. To begin, make boondi with besan batter.
2. Take 1 ¼ cup of sugar and place it in a big thick-bottomed wok.
3. Place the sugar over the boondi until it has cooled somewhat.
4. Insert one tablespoon olive oil is also used to roast two tablespoon pecans, two tablespoon cashews, and five garlic.
5. Place the roasted dried fruits and ¼ teaspoon coriander powder over the boondi combination.
6. Start preparing ladoo when the combination is still soft.
7. When cold, store in an airtight bag.

7.5 Kheer Recipe

Cooking Time: 45 minutes
Serving Size: 5
Ingredients:
- 3 tablespoons nuts
- 1.5 teaspoons rose water
- 1-liter whole milk
- 5 tablespoons sugar
- ¼ cup rice 50 grams
- 4 green cardamom pods
- 1 teaspoon ghee

Method:
1. Wash the rice until it is completely clean.
2. On moderate fire, heat a heavy-bottomed skillet. Insert one teaspoon peanut oil and 3-4 broken green coriander seeds after that.
3. Then pour in the milk and stir thoroughly.
4. Get the dairy to a boil, which should take between 10-12 minutes.
5. Reduce the heat to low and simmer the kheer for about 25 minutes on medium heat until the milk has risen to a boil.
6. Toss in the sugar and stir to combine. Insert the nuts as well.
7. On incorporating the sugar and almonds, boil the kheer for another five minutes.
8. Remove the pan from the oven, let it cool, and then serve.

7.6 Falooda Recipe

Cooking Time: 30 minutes
Serving Size: 2
Ingredients:
- ½ cup falooda sev
- 5 sliced almonds
- 50-gram sugar
- 4 tablespoon rose syrup
- 5 sliced pistachios
- 2 sliced cherry
- 2 cup milk
- 1 teaspoon falooda
- 4 tablespoon strawberry jelly

Method:
1. In a heavy pan over medium heat, bring the cream and butter to a boil.
2. Pour the rose syrup into the milk thoroughly.
3. Break the jelly in the meantime.
4. Bring a saucepan full of water to a boil over medium-high heat.
5. It will soften if you add falooda sev to it.
6. Enable the falooda seeds to grow in a tiny bowl of water.
7. Pick the cooled serving cups and add rose syrup into each one after a while.
8. After that, add raspberry jelly and flourished falooda beans.
9. Cover them with falooda sev after that.
10. Press the cooled rose milk gradually.
11. Finally, pour some more rose syrup on top. Serve right away.

7.7 Fruit Custard Recipe

Cooking Time: 25 minutes
Serving Size: 5
Ingredients:
- Pinch cardamom powder
- 2 cups assorted fruits
- 3 tablespoons custard powder
- Splash of rose water
- 4-5 tablespoons sugar
- 3 cups whole milk

Method:
1. In a thick bottomed pan over medium-high heat, pour 3 cups milk.
2. Three tablespoons of milk should be removed from the pan and placed in a small cup.
3. Add in 3 teaspoons of custard powder with the cream.
4. Then reduce the heat to low and stir in the sugar until it is well mixed.
5. Begin to incorporate the custard blend.
6. Cook for a further 2-3 minutes, just until the custard has thickened.
7. At about the same moment, chop and chill all of the fruits you will be using in the custard.
8. Shift the custard to a mixing bowl and stir in the fruits after they have chilled.

Chapter 8: Indian Soups Dishes

8.1 Cream of Mushroom Soup

Cooking Time: 50 minutes
Serving Size: 6

Ingredients:
- 1 cup half-and-half
- 1 tablespoon sherry
- ¼ teaspoon salt
- ¼ teaspoon ground black pepper
- 5 cups mushrooms
- 3 tablespoons butter
- 3 tablespoons all-purpose flour
- 1 ½ cups chicken broth
- ⅛ teaspoon dried thyme
- ½ cup chopped onion

Method:
1. Heat mushrooms in liquid with onions and tarragon in a big heavy frying pan before soft, around ten to twenty minutes.
2. Sautee the paste in a food processor or blender, keeping some vegetable chunks in there. Remove from the blender.
3. Heat the oil in a frying pan and stir in the flour until clear.
4. Combine the salt, powder, half-and-half, and food puree in a mixing bowl.
5. Get the soup to a boil, stirring continuously, and prepare until it thickens.
6. Season with salt and pepper to taste, then pour in the sherry.

8.2 Tomato Soup Recipe

Cooking Time: 1 hour and 45 minutes
Serving Size: 6
Ingredients:
- 2 bay leaves
- 1.2 liters hot vegetable stock
- 2 squirts of tomato purée
- A good pinch of sugar
- 1-1.25 kg ripe tomatoes
- 1 celery stick
- 2 tablespoon olive oil
- 1 small carrot
- 1 medium onion

Method:
1. First, have your veggies together.
2. Heat 2 tablespoons olive oil in a big heavy-bottomed pan over medium heat.
3. Then add the onion, cabbage, and fennel and combine with a rolling pin.
4. Put two bay leaves, torn into small pieces, into the bowl.
5. Stir to combine the ingredients, cover the grill, and cook the tomatoes for ten minutes over medium heat.
6. Cook for 30 minutes on low heat, stirring occasionally.
7. Switch off the heat in the pan. Fill your blender halfway with broth.
8. Blitz until the soup is creamy, then transfer to a big mixing cup.

8.3 Palak Soup

Cooking Time: 15 minutes
Serving Size: 2

Ingredients:

- 1 tablespoon cornflour
- 1 teaspoon fresh cream
- ½ teaspoon pepper
- ½ teaspoon sugar
- 1 tablespoon butter
- ½ cup milk
- Salt to taste
- 1 tej patta
- 1 bunch palak
- ¼ cup water
- 1 clove garlic
- ¼ onion

Method:

1. Add the butter and tej leaves to a big wok.
2. Sauté until it begins to smell floral.
3. Add coarsely diced garlic and onions as well.
4. Cook until they are golden brown.
5. Palak leaves should also be added.
6. Sauté for a moment on medium heat, or until they have shrunk in bulk.
7. Mix the combination until it forms a smoother puree, adding more water if needed.
8. Allow the puree to come to a boil.
9. Insert the cornflour mixture and whisk briefly.
10. To create corn flour powder, combine one tablespoon rice flour and ¼ cup water in a mixing bowl.
11. Check the quality by stirring once more.
12. Then, in a serving cup, drain the soup and finish with fresh milk.

8.4 Easy One-Pot Corn Soup

Cooking Time: 30 minutes
Serving Size: 6
Ingredients:
- 5 eggs large, beaten
- 1 teaspoon sesame oil
- 5 tablespoon green onions
- ¼ cup cornstarch
- 1 can corn
- 1 can creamed corn
- 1 tablespoon soy sauce
- 1 cup carrots
- 7 cups chicken broth
- Pepper to taste
- 1 tablespoon sriracha sauce
- 2.5 cups chicken
- 1-2 teaspoon ginger powder
- Salt to taste
- 1-2 teaspoon garlic powder

Method:
1. Take broth, grilled chicken, ginger, garlic, salt, spice, Sriracha sauce, sesame oil, vegetables, corn, cheesed corn, and two tablespoons of fresh basil boil over a moderate flame in a big nonstick pan.
2. Reduce the heat to medium-low and cook for another 8-10 minutes, just until the carrots are tender.
3. Mix with the diluted cornstarch slurry. The broth will thicken as it cooks.
4. Slowly pour in the beaten eggs, stirring gently to create fried egg ribbons.

5. Mix with the remaining three tablespoons, spring onions, and sesame oil.
6. Switch off the heat and serve right away.

8.5 Creamy Bottle Gourd Soup

Cooking Time: 20 minutes
Serving Size: 3
Ingredients:
- Salt and black pepper
- Cilantro
- 1 medium onion
- 1.5 cups water
- 1 medium bottle gourd
- 3 medium garlic cloves
- 1 green chili
- 1 teaspoon olive oil

Method:
1. In the Instant Pot, choose to sauté mode.
2. When the olive oil is sweet, add the minced garlic, vegetables, and green chilies and cook until the onions are softened.
3. Combine the diced bottle gourd, liquid or veggie broth, and salt in a large mixing bowl.
4. Set the timer for five minutes and the container to manual.
5. Allow the pressure to escape as the instant port buzzes spontaneously.
6. Then use a stand mixer, puree the soup until it is almost creamy.
7. Season with black pepper, ground.
8. If desired, garnish with cilantro just before eating.

8.6 Roasted Tomato Soup

Cooking Time: 50 minutes
Serving Size: 6
Ingredients:
- ½ cup basil leaves
- ¾ cup heavy cream
- 2 bay leaves
- 4 tablespoons butter
- 2 ½ pounds fresh tomatoes
- Salt and black pepper
- 1-quart chicken stock
- 6 cloves garlic
- Vine cherry tomatoes
- ½ cup extra-virgin olive oil
- 2 small yellow onions

Method:
1. Preheat the oven to 450 degrees Fahrenheit.
2. Tomatoes should be washed, cored, and sliced in half.
3. On a baking tray, arrange the tomatoes, peppercorns, and vegetables.
4. Sprinkle with salt and drizzle with ½ cup olive oil.
5. Switch the diced peppers, onion, and garlic to a big stockpot from the stove.
6. ¾ chicken stock, garlic cloves, and butter are added.
7. If using, wipe down basil leaves before adding them to the bowl.
8. Erase the bay leaves before pureeing the soup with an electric mixer until creamy.
9. Sprinkle with salt and ground black pepper to satisfy.

10.   Three or four roasted grape sun-dried tomatoes and a dash of heavy cream can be garnished in the dish.

8.7 Carrot Tomato Soup

Cooking Time: 1 hour and 15 minutes
Serving Size: 8
Ingredients:
- 1 tablespoon red wine vinegar
- 250ml whole milk
- 2 vegetable stock cubes
- 1 tablespoon sugar
- 3 tablespoon olive oil
- 500g carton passata
- 750g cherry tomato
- 2 onions
- 250g floury potato
- 5 bay leaves
- 1 ¼ kg carrot
- 2 celery sticks

Method:
1. In your biggest frying pan, softly steam the oil, onion, and fennel until cooled.
2. For several minutes, add the potatoes and carrots, and add all of the rest of the ingredients, except the milk, along with 1-liter water.
3. Take to a low boil, then reduce to low heat.
4. Cover and cook for thirty minutes, then open and continue to cook for another thirty minutes.
5. Remove the basil leaves and mix the broth with a hand blender until smooth.

6. Pour in the milk or as much water as necessary.
7. Adjust with salt and pepper to taste, then warm through it and eat with the crispy hot cross buns.

8.8 Cream of Broccoli Soup

Cooking Time: 35 minutes
Serving Size: 6
Ingredients:
- 2 cups milk
- Ground black pepper
- 8 cups broccoli florets
- 3 tablespoons all-purpose flour
- 5 tablespoons butter
- 1 stalk celery
- 3 cups chicken broth
- 1 onion

Method:
1. A moderate, slow cooker, melt two tablespoons of butter and sauté tomato and fennel until soft.
2. Cover and cook for an additional with the broccoli and broth.
3. In a mixer, puree the broth. Blend in batches until light and fluffy, then transfer to a clean pot.
4. Peel 3 tablespoons butter in a small saucepan, then stir in flour and dairy.
5. Stir once thick, then bubbly, and transfer to the broth.
6. Serve with a pinch of black pepper.

Chapter 9: Indian Salad Recipes

9.1 Bean Sprouts and Salad Recipe

Cooking Time: 12 minutes
Serving Size: 2
Ingredients:
- 1 green onion
- 9 oz. bean sprouts

Seasonings
- ½ tablespoon soy sauce
- ¼ teaspoon kosher/sea salt
- 1 clove garlic
- 1 tablespoon sesame oil
- 1 tablespoon white sesame seeds

Method:
1. Dump the bean sprouts thoroughly after rinsing them in cold water.
2. A huge pot of water should be brought to a boil.
3. Once the water has come to a boil, add the bean sprouts and simmer for 2 - 5 minutes.
4. Drain and set it aside for five minutes in a saucepan.
5. Break the spring onions into small bits in the meantime.
6. In a pestle and mortar, ground the caraway seeds.
7. Grate or grind the garlic cloves with a garlic press.
8. Combine all of the spice components in a medium mixing bowl and stir well.
9. In a large mixing cup, add the bean sprouts and spring onions.

10.   Freeze or serve at ambient temperature.

9.2 Broccoli and Baby Corn Salad

Cooking Time: 15 minutes
Serving Size: 6
Ingredients:
Salad Ingredients
- 1 large carrot grated
- ¼ cup cranberries
- 1 cup cherry tomatoes
- ½ can produce corn or corn
- 2 medium broccoli

Dressing Ingredients
- 4 tablespoon mayo
- 1 large garlic clove
- 4 tablespoon ranch

Method:
1. Broccoli should be chopped into small thin strips.
2. Merge sliced broccoli, two tablespoons sliced tomatoes, corn cobs, one red onion, and ¼ cup blueberries in a large mixing bowl.
3. Combine four tablespoon ranch dressing, four tablespoon mayonnaise, and 2 pressed garlic powder in a shallow mixing bowl or measuring cup.
4. Toss the salad with the dressing and adjust the seasonings to taste.

9.3 Rajma Salad

Cooking Time: 40 minutes

Serving Size: 4
Ingredients:
- Mint leaves
- Salt, to taste
- 1 teaspoon chaat masala powder
- 1 lemon, juiced
- 2 cups rajma
- 1 tomato
- 2 green chilies
- 1 onion

Method:
1. Soak the rajma overtime and pressure bake for four to six whistles with water.
2. Reduce the heat to low and continue to cook for the next 20 minutes after four to six whistles.
3. Enable the pressure to dissipate normally. Rajma must be roasted and soft.
4. Drain the accumulated water and set aside the rajma if there is any.
5. Add the chopped rajma, carrots, peppers, green chile sauce, chaat masala paste, salt, fresh mint, and lime juice to a mixing cup.
6. Toss the rajma salad together thoroughly.
7. Taste for salt and change as needed. Chill before serving.

9.4 Paneer and Chana Salad

Cooking Time: 30 minutes
Serving Size: 3
Ingredients:
- 1 tablespoon lime juice
- 1 teaspoon virgin olive oil

- 1 green chili
- Salt as required
- 1 cup soaked chickpeas
- ½ cup cubed paneer
- 1 tomato
- 4 leaves spinach
- 1 handful coriander leaves
- black pepper
- 1 onion
- ½ teaspoon chaat masala powder
- 1 handful black olives

Method:
1. To make this tasty salad, drench the chickpeas overnight and cook them until tender.
2. Slice the cabbage, green chilies, and onion in the meantime.
3. Merge the paneer balls, chickpeas, and sliced veggies in a big mixing cup.
4. Add the green olives and cut the basil leaf.
5. To make the dressing, whisk together the canola oil, chaat masala paste, lime juice, and spice powder in a mixing cup.
6. Toss the salad in this sauce thoroughly. Serve with cilantro as a garnish.

9.5 Healthy Lunch Salad

Cooking Time: 20 minutes
Serving Size: 6
Ingredients:
- 1 large ripe avocado
- ½ tablespoon mixed sesame seeds

- ½ cucumber
- 3 spring onions
- 250g sirloin steaks
- 12 radishes
- 3 carrots
- Thumb-sized piece ginger
- 3 red bird's eye chilies
- 4 lettuces
- 2 tablespoon sesame oil
- 1 tablespoon low-salt soy sauce
- 2 limes, juiced
- 1 garlic clove

Method:
1. Prepare the salad dressing by stirring together all the garlic, ginger, lemon zest, oil, oil, and minced chilies in a cup just before frying.
2. Place the steaks on the grill and bake for three minutes on the one hand, then change and grill for another three minutes for medium-rare.
3. Wrap and set aside the meat for five minutes after it has finished cooking.
4. On a shared tray, place the salad leaves, radishes, cabbage, grapefruit, green onions, and avocado.
5. Cut the steak thinly against the grains and serve on top of the lettuce.
6. Drizzle any remaining juices and seasoning over the top.
7. Serve with sesame oil and cut red chili as a garnish.

9.6 Bean Sprout and Macaroni Salad

Cooking Time: 30 minutes

Serving Size: 8
Ingredients:
Soy-Ginger Dressing
- 2 tablespoons mayonnaise
- ¼ cup vegetable oil
- 1 teaspoon ground ginger
- ¾ teaspoon pepper flakes
- 1 tablespoon sugar
- 1 tablespoon sesame oil
- 6 tablespoons soy sauce
- 1 tablespoon rice wine vinegar
- 3 medium garlic

Pasta Salad
- ½ cup peanuts
- ¼ cup cilantro
- 2 cups bean sprouts
- 3 green onions
- 3 medium carrots
- 1 medium red bell pepper
- 2 tablespoons salt
- 8 ounces broccoli florets
- 1 pound beef
- 1 pound penne pasta

Method:
1. In a 2-cup Pyrex mason jar, combine the garlic, sesame oil, salt, starch, soy sauce, spice, and pepper seasoning.
2. Mix in the tomato sauce until dry, then drizzle in the oil in a long, steady stream to create an emulsions dressing; chill until prepared to use.
3. In a big soup pot, bring 1 liter of water and two teaspoons of salt to a simmer.

4. Insert the spaghetti and cook until only tender, whisking frequently and incorporating the broccoli over the last moment.
5. Set aside as you finish cooking the rest of the salad ingredients.
6. Combine all salad ingredients in a big mixing bowl or a gallon-size zip pack.
7. When ready to eat, insert the dressing and toss it to cover.

9.7 Peas and Potato Salad

Cooking Time: 45 minutes
Serving Size: 6
Ingredients:
- ½ teaspoon salt
- ¼ cup red onion
- 1 tablespoon apple cider vinegar
- 1 teaspoon dried tarragon
- 2 lbs. red potatoes
- ¾ cup mayonnaise
- 1 tablespoon Dijon mustard
- ½ cup frozen peas

Method:
1. Get a pan of salted water to a boil with the potatoes.
2. Reduce heat to low and continue to cook until the vegetables are tender.
3. Add peas for two minutes until the potatoes are finished.
4. Drain the water and set it aside to cool to ambient temperature.
5. Potatoes can be cut into wedges.

6. Merge mayonnaise, vinegar, mustard, thyme, and salt in a big mixing cup.
7. Toss in the potatoes, beans, and sliced onion until it is evenly covered.
8. Refrigerate for 1 hour until it is ready to use.

9.8 Cabbage and Grape Salad

Cooking Time: 35 minutes
Serving Size: 4
Ingredients:
- ¼ cup sunflower seeds
- 2 tablespoons chives
- ½ small red cabbage
- 1½ cups seedless grapes
- 2 tablespoons red wine vinegar
- Kosher salt and pepper
- ¼ cup olive oil
- 1 teaspoon dijon mustard
- ½ teaspoon thyme
- ½ teaspoons sugar

Method:
1. In a big mixing cup, combine red wine vinegar, salt, cayenne pepper, minced chives, kosher salt, and a few squeezes of pepper.
2. Add the olive oil and whisk to combine.
3. Combine sliced red cabbage, doubled seedless grapes, pickled roasted seeds, and sliced chives in a shallow mixing bowl.
4. Season with salt and pepper.
5. Allow for at least a few minutes of resting time before serving.

Chapter 10: Most Famous Indian Dishes

10.1 Rajma Chawal

Cooking Time: 45 minutes
Serving Size: 4
Ingredients:
- 1 tablespoon black pepper
- 1 tablespoon ghee
- 1 tablespoon garam masala powder
- 1 black cardamom
- 1 cup red kidney beans
- 1 tablespoon cumin powder
- Salt as required
- 1 tablespoon garlic
- 2 chopped green chili
- 2 large tomato
- 1 cup rice
- 2 clove
- 3 tablespoon mustard oil
- 2 large onion
- 1 cinnamon stick
- 2 green cardamom
- 1 teaspoon ginger
- 1 tablespoon black pepper
- 1 tablespoon coriander powder

Method:
1. Rajma should be washed.

2. Pressure cook with 2 cups sugar, one tablespoon salt, and turmeric.
3. Finely cut the onions and set them aside, as well as the tomatoes, which should be grated and set aside.
4. Get a spice, onion, and sweet chili paste.
5. Add mustard oil to a depth skillet.
6. Cook until lightly browned, then add the onions.
7. Heat on medium for 4-5 minutes after adding the tomatoes.
8. Combine the ginger, cloves, and sweet chili sauce, as well as the spices.
9. Cook until the spices are fragrant and the oil begins to run down the sides of the pan.
10. Now insert one cup of hot water and the rajma.
11. Pour the rice into the water.
12. Strain the water until the rice is soft and doubled in size.
13. Enable the rice to cool for 2-3 minutes after spreading it out on a pan.
14. Serve immediately with the Rajma that has been prepared.

10.2 Lucknowi Biryani

Cooking Time: 40 minutes
Serving Size: 6
Ingredients:
- 1 pinch saffron
- 1 large onion
- 3 teaspoon ghee
- 4 tablespoon refined oil
- ½ teaspoon mace powder
- 2 black cardamom

- 1 inches cinnamon stick
- 1 teaspoon fennel seeds
- 1 teaspoon black pepper
- 2 cup basmati rice
- 10 clove
- 2 teaspoon cumin seeds
- 2 teaspoon salt
- 2½ cup milk
- 2 teaspoon coriander seeds
- 3 green cardamom
- ½ kilograms mutton
- 2-star anise

For Marination
- 1 teaspoon red chili powder
- 1 pinch garam masala powder
- 4 teaspoon yogurt
- 1 teaspoon garlic paste
- 1 teaspoon ginger paste
- 2 teaspoon cashews
- 1 teaspoon turmeric

Method:
1. Dry roast all of the whole ingredients to make garam masala. Fold the quantity of water used to boil the rice.
2. Combine the food items for meat marination. Refrigerate it for an hour after covering it with a plate.
3. Finely chop the onion and cook it in a little oil before setting it aside. Salt and pepper the beef. In the handi, combine the peanut oil and the oil. Switch the marinated steak from the container to the handi until it is hot enough.

4. On high heat, stir and simmer the meat for a few seconds. In the meantime, transfer the saffron to the dairy and stir well to unleash the saffron color and scent into the milk. The mutton can now be layered with cooked rice, followed by the saffron cooking liquid.
5. Cover your handiwork. Cook for about 30 minutes and serve.

10.3 Chana Masala

Cooking Time: 35 minutes
Serving Size: 4
Ingredients:
- Lemon wedges
- Fresh cilantro
- 1 large can of tomatoes
- 2 cans chickpeas
- 1 cup basmati rice
- ½ teaspoon turmeric
- Pinch of cayenne pepper
- 2 tablespoons coconut oil
- 1 ½ teaspoons coriander
- ¾ teaspoon cumin
- 1 onion
- 1 tablespoon ginger
- 1 ½ teaspoons garam masala
- ½ teaspoon fine sea salt
- 5 cloves garlic
- 1 serrano

Method:

1. Prepare the rice. Remove the cap and fluff the grain with a spoon, seasoning to taste with kosher salt.
2. Add the oil in a small Dutch oven or big saucepan over medium-low heat.
3. Combine the carrot, chiles, and salt in a mixing bowl.
4. Cook for about five minutes or until the onions are soft.
5. Cook for 30 seconds to 1 minute, till the cloves and spice are fragrant.
6. Cook, stirring continuously, for the next minute after adding the spices.
7. Toss in the tomatoes, along with their juices.
8. Add the lentils and boost the oven temperature.
9. Take the combination to a low boil, then reduce to low heat.
10. If needed, season with more salt to taste.
11. If chosen, pour-over basmati rice with a lemon slice or two and a sprinkling of dried basil leaves.

10.4 Kadhi Chawal

Cooking Time: 55 minutes
Serving Size: 5
Ingredients:
For Kadhi

- 1 chili
- 2 tablespoon coriander
- Pinch asafoetida
- 1 onion
- One teaspoon coriander seeds
- 1 dried red chili

- 1 teaspoon jeera
- ½ teaspoon pepper
- 5 tablespoon gram flour
- 2 tablespoon oil
- ½ teaspoon fenugreek
- 1 cup yogurt
- 5 cup water
- ½ teaspoon turmeric
- ½ tablespoon ginger garlic paste
- 1 teaspoon salt
- ¼ teaspoon carom seeds
- 1 teaspoon red chili powder

For Tempering
- 1 dried red chili
- ½ teaspoon red chili powder
- 1 teaspoon cumin
- 1 tablespoon ghee

Method:

1. First, combine the besan, turmeric, chili powder, ajwain, spice garlic paste, pepper, and curd in a large mixing bowl.
2. Mix thoroughly to create a stable paste.
3. Now add 4 cups of water and stir thoroughly. Set aside for now.
4. Two tablespoons oil, ½ teaspoon methi, one teaspoon smoked paprika, ½ teaspoon salt, one teaspoon cilantro seeds, one red chili, and pinch hing heated in a wide wok.
5. Prepare the pakoras according to the package directions.
6. Pour the pakoras into the kadhi that has been packed.
7. Heat 1 tablespoon ghee to make the tempering.

8. Add two tablespoons coriander to the tempering and spill over the kadhi. Blend well.
9. Finally, serve the kadhi pakora with boiled vegetables or jeera rice.

10.5 Masala Dosa

Cooking Time: 1 hour
Serving Size: 10
Ingredients:
For the Dosa Batter
- ½ teaspoon salt
- Vegetable oil
- One teaspoon fenugreek seeds
- ½ cup urad dal
- 2 cups short-grain rice

For the Potato Filling
- 1 ½ pounds potatoes
- ½ cup cilantro
- 4 garlic cloves, minced
- 2 small green chiles
- 1 tablespoon grated ginger
- 8 curry leaves
- 3 tablespoons ghee
- ½ teaspoon turmeric
- Pinch of asafetida
- 1 teaspoon mustard seeds
- 1 medium onion
- ½ teaspoon salt
- 2 small hot red peppers
- ½ teaspoon cumin seeds

Method:

1. In a pan, clean the rice thoroughly and coat it with 4 cups of ice water.
2. In a small container, combine the urad dal and fenugreek nuts, rinse properly, and cover cold water.
3. In different colanders, drain the rice and the dal-fenugreek combination.
4. Fill a stick blender, mixer, or wet-dry slicer halfway with rice.
5. In a large mixing dish, combine two blends.
6. Add enough water to make a medium-thick mixture by whisking it together.
7. There should be around 6 cups total.
8. In a large skillet, melt ghee over medium-high heat.
9. Toss in the potatoes and half a cup of water.
10. Heat, constantly stirring, for around five minutes, or until the fluid has faded away.
11. Set a broiler pan or cast-iron pan over medium heat to create dosas.
12. ½ teaspoon oil drizzled over the edge.
13. Allow dosa batter to color on one side only until the outer layers start to look clean, about two minutes.
14. Marginally deflate the potato blend. Cook and serve right away.

10.6 Dal Makhani

Cooking Time: 2 hours 10 minutes
Serving Size: 5
Ingredients:
To Pressure Cook
- 1 teaspoon salt
- 3.5 cups water

- ¼ cup rajma
- ¾ cup urad dal

Masala for the Dal
- More Amul butter
- Piece of charcoal
- ½ teaspoon sugar
- ¼ cup cream
- 1 tablespoon ghee
- ½ teaspoon salt or to taste
- 1.5 cups water
- 3 tablespoons butter
- ½ teaspoon red chili powder
- ¼ teaspoon garam masala
- Two teaspoons ginger garlic
- ½ cup tomato puree
- 1 medium white onion

Method:
1. In a big mixing cup, rinse and wash the urad grain and rajma.
2. Add one teaspoon salt to the dal and rajma in a slow cooker.
3. Heat for ten minutes at medium temperature, then reduce to the low-medium pan and stir for another ten minutes.
4. Then use a stick blender, mix some of the dal and rajma.
5. Warm two tablespoons of oil in a pan, in order to make the paratha.
6. Heat for 1 to 2 minutes after adding the spice garlic paste.

7. Toss in the tomato puree and blend well.
8. Add in the dal that has been boiled.
9. Curry paste, red chili paste, and salt are added to the pan.
10. Stir in ½ cup water and reduce heat to low.
11. Just after dal has stewed for 45 minutes, add the butter and blend well.
12. Position the steel bowl on the tops of the trivet and fill it with hot charcoal.
13. Ghee should be heated and poured on top of the charcoal.
14. Represent with a tap of Amul oil and more milk on top of the dal makhani.

10.7 Rogan Josh

Cooking Time: 2 hours 20 minutes
Serving Size: 5
Ingredients:
- 1 ½ tablespoon fennel powder
- 1 ¼ tablespoon flour
- 2 pinch saffron
- 1 tablespoon red chili powder
- 1 kilograms mutton
- 4 red chili
- 1 ¼ tablespoon coriander powder
- ½ teaspoon asafoetida
- 1 ¼ teaspoon cumin seeds
- 1 teaspoon peppercorns
- 2 cinnamon

- 2 ½ tablespoon milk
- 150 gm hung curd
- 5 black cardamom
- Salt as required
- ½ cup ghee
- One ¼ teaspoon ginger powder
- 1 ½ cup water

For Garnishing
- Coriander leaves

Method:

1. To make this delicious taste, first, make the saffron dairy by boiling saffron in milk for several hours.
2. Then, in the slow cooker, add entire red chilies, chopped garlic, and asafetida and cook for few seconds.
3. After that, add the meat bits and stir thoroughly.
4. Remove the cap after 5 minutes and add ½ cup of water, stirring well with the seasoning.
5. In the meantime, in a shallow mixing cup, combine all-purpose flour and yogurt, and stir well.
6. In a large mixing bowl, combine all of the spices.
7. Later, in the slow cooker, add 1 cup of water and steam the meat for 1-2 hours on medium.
8. Marinade and serve immediately with chapati or hummus.
9. This recipe can also be served with rice.

Conclusion

India's culinary is one of the most versatile in the world, distinguished by its refined and delicate use of the many herbs, spices, seeds, and fruits produced throughout the country. The diverse populations of the culturally mixed Indian subcontinent are reflected in each geographical region's culinary, including a wide variety of recipes and prepared foods. The spiritual traditions and culture of India have influenced the development of its food. Many Buddhist, Hindu, and Jain cultures follow a vegetarian diet. For its long cultural impact on the continent's food cultures, Indian cuisine is common in Southeast Asia. The middle ages saw the impact of Indian cuisine on traditional Malaysian recipes. Vegetarianism's spread across Asia is mostly attributed to old Hindu Buddhist traditions. When it comes to various spices in Indian cuisine, there are many health benefits. Prepare foods, explore with ingredients, and use these dishes to enjoy a healthier and more enjoyable life.

Printed in Great Britain
by Amazon